# A Brief History of
# Western Culture and Philosophy

### HIROMICHI NISHINO

RYUTSU KEIZAI UNIVERSITY PRESS

# MAP OF EUROPE

① Copenhagen
② NETHERLANDS
③ BELGIUM
④ LUXEMBOURG
⑤ SWITZERLAND
⑥ AUSTRIA
⑦ CZECH
⑧ SLOVAKIA

⑨ HANGARY
⑩ SERBIA
⑪ BULGARIA
⑫ NORTH MACEDONIA
⑬ ALBANIA
⑭ Istanbul
⑮ Athens
⑯ LEBANON

⑰ ISRAEL
⑱ JORDAN
⑲ KUWAIT
⑳ TURKMENISTAN
㉑ AFGHANISTAN
㉒ PAKISTAN

# CONTENTS

# INTRODUCTION

What is the purpose of learning? Is it to enrich our lives by developing science and technology? Is it to create a better and more democratic state and an equal and free society? Is it to establish a means of communication between people by learning a language? Some people may say that all such things are not true and that all the knowledge acquired through learning is for the purpose of making money. Others may say that they turn to learning in order to satisfy their intellectual curiosity that overflows from within, purely wanting to ascertain the truth.

However, all of the benefits that learning brings to humanity mentioned above are different from the original purpose of learning and are just by-products. If I were to describe the true purpose of learning, it would be to "acquire the ability to think for oneself." By learning, people cultivate a mind of self-discipline and even ask themselves how they are and what they should be. We do not just take the ideas and laws preached by great historical figures and the words of our teachers. It is not a matter of memorizing the entire contents written in the textbook. Determining what is right and what is wrong with one's own mind is the essence of learning. That is why there are experiments in science classes at school. For example, we learned in school that the speed of an object falling is not related to its weight, but we should not accept that it must be true because it was said by a great man named Galileo Galilei. Galileo apparently proved this law by dropping a large ball and a small ball from the Leaning Tower of Pisa, showing the two spheres falling to the ground at the same time. If you feel that this law is in doubt, you can do the same experiment to confirm it. No matter how famous or genius Galileo was, that is not a basis for believing in his theory. No matter how great his teachings are, you can doubt them. Therefore, the essence of learning is "thinking for oneself and making one's own decisions." Also, when we study history, politics, and economics, we must not be satisfied with just knowing what happened in the past of human society and how the current state works. After taking a bird's-eye view of history and understanding current politics, we learned for the first time by thinking for ourselves about how society should change in the future. Similarly, literature and mathematics are aimed at "thinking for oneself." As we learn in this way, we will eventually realize that various fields of study influence each other. The development of science shakes up the state system, giving birth to a new country. Changes in politics give rise to new ideas and morals, and artists inspired by new ways of thinking create works that have never been seen before. We will realize that a wide variety of academic disciplines are intricately related and influence each other, causing reactions, and all of them are connected to our own wisdom.

Considering how the knowledge we acquired from studing natural sciences shaped ourselves. Use the hints of history and politics to think about how we should live and do our duty. Through literature, think about why we live. In this way, we will refer to all kinds of academic disciplines, clarify how the world works, and think about ourselves on our own. We call this kind of study "philosophy."

Looking back on human history, we see many wars caused by religious conflicts. People fought each other because of differences in the gods they believed in and their doctrines, and many crises and tragedies occurred. But in the 16$^{th}$ century, people put an end to those days when such religions dominated both the state and the minds of the people. Since modern times, what people believe in the world has changed from religion to science. The Ptolemaic theory was denied, and it became common knowledge that the earth is moving. Technology has made remarkable strides; capitalism spread with the Industrial Revolution in the 18$^{th}$ century, the influence of religion waned, and in the 19$^{th}$ century, Nietzsche even left the words "God died." Since then, the misfortunes of mankind have continued. There are many world wars: the First and Second World Wars, the Cold War, the Vietnam War, and the Gulf War. Conflicts around the world never cease. After the US-Soviet confrontation, tension between the U.S. and China has increased. In society, we have many problems to resolve, for example, the loss of employment due to the development of AI, the scramble between nations for limited resources, and we also remember the "9/11 terrorist attack" that occurred in New York City in 2001 and the "3/11 earthquake" that occurred in East Japan in 2011 with the serious nuclear power plant accident. Over the past three years, the Corona pandemic has afficted the world endlessly, and the Russian invasion of Ukraine began in February 2022, showing no signs of ending.

Popular novels, on the other hand, try to dissolve loneliness in modern society. Sometimes, however, superficial novels only stir up the emotions of young people, deny tradition and common sense, and appeal for spiritual freedom from preconceived notions. The novel is limited to personal experience, depicts only a very limited and small world, and does not take a bird's-eye view of the complex and diverse modern society. From there, we seldom receive any new messages or visions.

Unfortunately, modern people tend to avoid a head-on confrontation with the question, "Why do we live here, and why do we live now?" and develop only science and technology without thinking about justice, coexistence with nature, the weight of life, etc. Nuclear power possessed by mankind might be a weapon of destruction that will destroy the entire world. While holding it in hand, humanity does not know its purpose or how to use it. Now is the time for us to become familiar with philosophy and to acquire the ability to think deeply again. In order to do so, we first need to have a firm grasp of the outline of the history of Western philosophy. At the same time, I would like the readers of this book to have a firm understanding of Greek mythology in the precursor to the establishment of Greek philosophy and also to consider the story of the Bible, which replaced philosophy in the Middle Ages and had a great influence on the psyche of Westerners. This book also explains the brief history of the countries in which each great philosopher and even notable thinker was born and raised, as a prologue to each story, and helps readers to understand the great person. Isn't it necessary now more than ever to philosophize in order to prepare for an uncertain era, to respond to the changes of the turbulent times, and to discern the essence of the changes in the world? As the author of this book, I would be very happy if you could read this one as an introduction to the history of Western philosophy.

# 1. Before Greek Philosophy

## Mesopotamian Civilization

On the spreading plains of sedimentary fertile soils between the Tigris and Euphrates rivers, approximately 5,500 BC, the Sumerians founded the world's oldest agricultural civilization (The agricultural civilization of the Yellow River and Yangtze River basins in China began from 4,000 BC to 3,000 BC, and the Indus Valley civilization, which originated in the Indus River basin of India, began around 2,600 BC). After that, through the Ubaid culture (around 5,300 BC), the Uruk culture (around 4,000 BC), and others, dynasties flourished mainly in southern Babylonia (present-day southern Iraq) from 1,894 BC to 539 BC. And other various dynasties flourished. However, in the 4th century BC, those areas became part of the Hellenistic (Greek) world due to the expedition of Alexander the Great. In the 16th century, those areas became part of the Ottoman Empire, and after World War I, the current Iraq region was under British mandate. Then, it became independent from Britain, and the Kingdom of Iraq was established (1932-58). A military coup d'état in 1958 led to the establishment of the Republic of Iraq.

In 1979, the country became the dictatorship of Saddam Hussein (1937-2006). The Iran-Iraq War (1980-88), the Gulf War (January-March 1991), which began with Iraq's invasion of Kuwait in

Enki, the Sumerian god

Ziggurat of Ur, Iraq

August 1990, and the Iraq War, which lasted from March 2003 to December 2011, have caused the destruction or loss of many Mesopotamian civilization sites. In such a situation, the ancient city of Babylon was registered as a UNESCO World Cultural Heritage Site in 2019. It is said that alphabets were invented by the Sumerians around 2,000 BC under the influence of the writing system of their own cuneiform characters and Egyptian hieroglyphs. Alphabets first appeared in present-day Palestine or the Middle East, then widely used in the Greco-Roman world, and after all, they were introduced to Europe. Similarities between Sumerian literature and early Greek mythology have been pointed out, so it is possible that Greek mythology was born under the influence of Sumerian culture.

## Egyptian civilization

Egyptian civilization is thought to have begun around 5,000-4,000 BC. The ancient Egyptians settled and farmed on the fertile banks of the Nile. In the beginning, a number of tribal states existed, but eventually they were united, and the ancient Egyptian dynasty began around 3,000 BC. Most of the country was desert, and cultures developed in the upper and lower reaches of the Nile River basin. The dynasty ruled both of them. The capital was Memphis, and the oldest pyramid in Egypt (Pyramid of Djoser) was built in the nearby cemetery of Saqqara (Memphis necropolis). The pyramid was completed in 2648 BC.

Tutankhamun (reigned 1332-23 BC?) was a pharaoh of the 18th dynasty of ancient Egypt. As a tragic king who ascended the throne at the age of 8 and died at the young age of 18, he is the most popular of all the Egyptian kings. Tutankhamun is also famous for the discovery of his golden death mask as one of his funeral goods. Cleopatra VII (r. 51-30 BC) tried to keep Egypt independent by communicating with the powerful men of the Roman Empire, such as Julius Caesar and Marcus Antonius. However, Antonius was defeated by the Roman army led by Caesar's adopted son Augustus. After all, Cleopatra committed suicide, and Egypt became one of the Roman provinces. From 1882 to 1922, Egypt was ruled by the British, but then became independent and became the Kingdom of Egypt, the Republic of Egypt, the United Arab Republic, and from 1971 (to the present), the Arab Republic of Egypt. Cairo has been the capital since the 7th century. Egypt has become one of the Arab countries, one of the countries of the Muslim world. The ancient Greeks are said to have learned geometry, mathematics, and science from the Egyptians.

Speaking of exhibits at the British Museum in London, Rosetta Stone is probably the foremost. It is on display in an ancient Egyptian gallery. In 1799, when Napoleon Bonaparte (1769-1821) led his army on an expedition to Egypt, Lieutenant Pierre-François discovered a 762-kilogram granite megalith in Rosetta, the Nile Delta. It was confirmed that the stone was a monument of an edict issued by one of the Egyptian kings in 196 BC. At that time, the French army was accompanied by a large number of archaeologists during the Egyptian expedition,

Rosetta Stone

Israel in Egypt

who collected art and artifacts from ancient Egypt and brought them back to France (they were largely returned to Egypt in 1816 after Napoleon's defeat). The Rosetta Stone was naturally supposed to be brought back to France, but the French were defeated by the British, who landed in Egypt, and in 1801, the Rosetta Stone was handed over to the British. The reason why this megalith is so important is that the surface of the stone monument was engraved with three different types of languages. That is: ancient Egyptian characters, Egyptian folk characters, and Greek characters. Because the same content was written in three different scripts, it was possible for the first time to decipher the ancient Egyptian hieroglyphs that no one had understood before. As a result, ancient Egyptology made a phenomenal academic development. The magnitude of the academic value of this stone is even romantic. In 1802, under the direction of King George III, the stone was donated to the British Museum and opened to the public. Since then, it has been the most popular exhibit to this day. Meanwhile, since 2003, when the British Museum celebrated its 250th anniversary, Egypt has been asking for the stone to be returned. Does this come to a conclusion? For example, what about acknowledging that the stone is owned by Egypt and displaying it at the British Museum with Egypt's consent? This will make more people around the world more interested in and know the ancient Egyptian civilization.

The Citadel of Cairo, a medieval Islamic-era fortifications in Egypt

# 2. A Brief History of Greece

The history of mankind began in Central Africa, then moved north, settled in Egypt, and then further north, toward present-day Iraq, India, and China, and on the other side, to present-day Turkey and Greek islands, and then to Western Europe. And prehistoric people built an advanced civilization in each region.

If we focus on Western history, ancient Greece is the cradle of all Western civilizations. The ancient Greeks learned from the Mesopotamian and Egyptian civilizations, inherited them, and developed themselves. In ancient Greece, city-states (poleis) such as Athens and Sparta, which were born from 800 BC to 500 BC, were established in various places, and there was no unified state until it was conquered by the Kingdom of Macedonia. Latin, which is said to be the root of Western languages, is derived from *Graecia*, which means "land of the Greeks." Geographically, Greece looks west to present-day western Europe and east to the Middle East and Asia. The ancient Greeks gained enormous wealth from trade and colonized Naples, Marseille, Alexandria, and other areas of the Mediterranean.

Parthenon

The small, dark-skinned ancient Greeks greatly promoted freedom and democracy through increased citizen political participation. They loved history, mathematics, sculpture, literature, theater, aesthetics, and philosophy, and they had a great influence on European civilization.

Mount Olympus, the highest peak in Greece, is 2,917 meters above sea level and has been considered sacred since ancient times and has given birth to various myths. The Acropolis of Athens was built on a lime hill 150 meters above sea level, and was a place dedicated to Athena, the ancient Greek goddess of wisdom, one of gods of Olympus. In the center of the hill there was the Parthenon (completed in 432 BC), a building built to worship Athena, the patron goddess of the city. Many of the sculptures that adorned the temple are now on display in the British Museum under the name Parthenon Marbles (formerly known as the Elgin Marbles). *Polis* originally meant "hill," "fort," or "city," and it came to mean "fortified city." *Acropolis* means a citadel with a temple on a rocky hill in the center of the fortified city.

The origins of the stories of gods and heroes, known as Greek mythology, are said to date back to around 1,500 BC. At that time, there was no written language and it was passed down orally. Some of the mythological masterpieces were Homer's epic poems, the *Iliad* and the *Odyssey*, which began to be recorded in written form around 900 BC.

Homer

Alexander the Great (356-323 BC), who became king of the Kingdom of Macedonia at the age of 20, built a great empire that stretched from Greece to North Africa and northwest India by

Alexander the Great

the age of 30. He decided to place his capital in Egypt and named it Alexandria. It is still the second largest city in Egypt after Cairo. Through Alexander the Great's expedition to the East (which destroyed the Persian Empire), Greek culture spread and Hellenism was formed. Hellenism is a word derived from the ancestor of the Greeks, "Hellen" (the Greeks=the Hellens), and later refers to a Greek culture, and then refers to a fusion of Greek culture and ancient Oriental culture. These days, the term Hellenism sometimes refers to the pursuit of art, humanity, and knowledge in contrast to Hebraism (monotheism, revelation, prophecy, precepts, eschatology) rooted in Judaism and Christianity.

In 146 BC, Greece was defeated by the Roman army and became one of the provinces of the Roman Empire. Eventually, the center of civilization shifted to Rome. In the $2^{nd}$ century AD, Emperor Hadrian was particularly fond of Greek culture and built the Temple of Zeus. In 395, when the Roman Empire was divided into East and West, the Greek region belonged to the Eastern Roman Empire (Byzantine Empire). The empire made Constantinople (a new city founded by Constantine I) as its imperial capital. However, it is thought that this empire was dominated by Greeks. In 620 AD, the official language changed from Latin to Greek.

The Greek region was later weakened by Slavic invasions (between the $5^{th}$ and $6^{th}$ centuries) and settlement of the Slavs (between the $7^{th}$ and $8^{th}$ centuries). In addition, there were Arab invasions in the $9^{th}$ century. In those days, the *polis* became known as the *kastron* and was transformed into a walled city known for its strong walled defenses. In 1204, a crusader expedition captured Constantinople, and the Eastern Roman Empire collapsed. Subsequently, crusader states such as the Kingdom of Serbia and the Duchy of Athens were established. From 1223 to 1299, the state was invaded by the Mongol Empire. In 1261, the Eastern Roman Empire was reestablished, but in 1453 Constantinople was destroyed by the Ottoman Empire. Thereafter, Turks (the Ottoman Empire) continued to rule the area. Constantinople is now called Istanbul, which is Turkey's largest city.

In 1821, the Greek War of Independence (of the Ottoman Empire) began. Greece officially became independent as the Kingdom of Greece in 1832. In 1924, a coup d'état led to a republican state, but in 1935, the monarchy was restored.

During World War II, Greece was invaded by Germany, Italy, and Bulgaria and was divided and ruled by three countries. After the war, Greece was liberated from the Axis forces, and a civil war broke out in 1946. The Soviet-backed communist forces and the U.S.-backed royalist government fought each other. And the communist forces were defeated in 1949. Later, when the United States tolerated a military coup, the king went into exile in Rome in 1967, and Greece became a military dictatorship. In the 1970s, the domestic economy became worse, and the government suppressed large-scale protests by university students, resulting in many deaths. As a result, the military dictatorship collapsed.

Later, the New Democracy Party (Nea Dimokratia) became the ruling party, the monarchy was officially abolished, and Greece became a republic. In the 1980s, it became a socialist government, but in 2010, it was discovered that a huge budget deficit was hidden, which led to a financial crisis, and the New Democracy Party won in the 2019 election, and the far-left government was gone. In 2021, they built a 40-kilometer-long wall along the border with Turkey not to allow immigrants and refugees from Syria, Afghanistan, Iraq, and other countries to come in via Turkey. The unemployment rate is still over 50%. The people of Greece are neither Catholic nor Protestant, but they are followers of the Greek Orthodox Church (97% of the population).

Located on the Mediterranean coast, Greece has a temperate climate, dry land, and rugged terrain. Agriculture includes cattle, sheep, goats, and pigs, as well as olives, grapes, and other fruits (olives are the third largest producer in the world). The main industries are shipping and tourism, and there are also mining industries (the world's fourth-largest producer of coal).

The ruins of the Parthenon on the Acropolis of Athens are probably the most representative symbolic sites of ancient Greece that we can see today. Of course, the ruins are a world cultural heritage site. From such a region, a country with such a deep history, Greek mythology was born, and three great philosophers, Socrates, Plato, and Aristotle, who valued human freedom, equality, and reason above all else, were produced.

# 3. Greek Mythology

Greek mythology is a tale of gods and heroes that has been handed down since around 1,500 BC. The gods depicted in Homer's *Iliad* and *Odyssey* were created in the image of man and possessed supreme power and beauty, but at the same time, they also had shortcomings and weaknesses.

On the summit of Olympus, they created a society of gods (12 Olympian gods: 6 male gods and 6 goddesses), but the gods were sometimes capricious, struggled for power with each

Twelve Olympians

other, fell in love, had adultery, and deceived each other. However, unlike human heroes, they had eternal life. In order not to be manipulated by these imperfect gods, it is possible that a philosophy was born that pursued a method of explaining the complex phenomena of the world and a rational way of thinking.

## Zeus

Zeus is a child born to Cronus and Rhea of the Titan gods. In Roman mythology, Zeus is called *Jupiter*. He is the god of Olympus and the father of mankind, as well as the guardian and ruling god. It can be said that he was a king among gods, with a majesty befitting an omniscient and almighty god. As a sky god, he ruled over clouds, rain, snow, and thunder. Zeus' holy beast is an eagle, and his holy tree is an orc. To interpret the oracle of Zeus, listen to the rustle of leaves on an oak tree. His father, Cronos, feared that he would be usurped by his own son in the future, because he had fought with his father Uranus and usurped the throne, and he swallowed the children born one after another. When Zeus was born, his mother Rhea wrapped the stone in her maternity clothes and gave it to Cronus to swallow. Zeus, who fled to the island of Crete (the largest and most populous of Greek islands) and grew up in a cave there. When he came of age, Zeus gave Cronus an emetic pill to spit out and resurrect his brothers and sisters to life. Zeus began a war for control with his brothers and sisters, who wanted to take revenge on their father. In this great war, the Titan gods were defeated and sealed in Tartarus, the deep abyss of the universe. Zeus ruled the heavenly world, Poseidon ruled the seas, and Hades became the lord of the underworld.

Zeus

His first wife, Metis (the goddess of wisdom), was wise and courageous, and Athena was their daughter. But before Athena was born, Zeus was told by Gaia (A goddess who symbolizes the earth) that the male god born between Zeus and Metis would surpass his father, so Zeus provoked Metis to turn into water if she can transform into anything, and when the pregnant Metis turned into water, Zeus drank it up. This story is reminiscent of *Puss in Boots*, in which the main character cat transforms an ogre into a mouse and eats it. But then Zeus had a severe headache, so he ordered his vassals to smash his head with an axe to find out the cause, and Athena, an armed woman, jumped out. Because Athena was not a male god but a goddess, Gaia's prophecy was no longer valid (This story is reminiscent of *Macbeth* by Shakespeare in which Macbeth received a prophecy that he cannot be killed by any man born of woman, but Macduff escaped the prophecy because he was born by cesarean section). Zeus adored Athena. On the other hand, Metis, who was swallowed by Zeus, became the wisdom and courage of Zeus, So, Zeus gained all the wisdom and all the abilities of Metis.

Later, while Zeus was married to Themis, he approached her sister Hera (the goddess of marriage, women, and family), divorced Themis, and married Hera. The jealous Hera then kept constant watch over Zeus' love affairs and inflicted harsh punishments on his mistresses and their children. Zeus continued to associate with many goddesses and human women, and had many children. When he mingled with goddesses or human women, he often transformed into another form such as a cuckoo or a bull. The child he had with a human woman became a demigod and a hero. Hercules is probably the most representative of these children. The story of Zeus having many human women bear children later led to many royal families in the Mediterranean region claiming that their ancestors were the children of Zeus.

Furthermore, the immediate cause of the 10-year Trojan War, known for

Achilles, the Greek hero who killed many Trojans, was the argument of the three goddesses (Hera, Athena, and Aphrodite) for the right to a golden apple engraved with the words "To the Most Beautiful Woman." However, it is said that this war, which caused many deaths, was also the intention of Zeus, who wanted to reduce the population of the human race that had increased too much on the earth through war. The ancient Olympic Festival, held every four years, was a celebration of the honor of Zeus. In Athens, a huge temple dedicated to Zeus (Temple of Zeus) was built by Emperor Hadrian.

## Europa

Europa was born as the daughter of the king of the ancient city of Tyrus (modern-day Lebanon). She grew up beautiful. When Zeus saw her one day, he fell in love with her immediately, transformed himself into a white bull to catch her off guard, and approached her while she was picking flowers. Playfully she straddled a white bull, which carried her away and took her across the sea to the

island of Crete. Then, Zeus returned to his original god form, and she was united to him. Europa became the first queen of Crete and they had three sons: Minos, Rhadamanthus, and Sarpedon. Zeus again took the form transformed back into a bull and soared into the starry sky, becoming the constellation Taurus (the Bull). The western region where Europa rode the bull and traveled was later called "Europe" in honor of her name.

Europa on the Bull (=Zeus)

## Athena

Possessed of beauty and wisdom (or strategy), Athena was worshipped as the goddess of war and the patroness of the fortified city, Athens. She was also the goddess in charge of the art of weaving. The sacred bird that conjures up the image of her is an owl, and the serpent, which represents wisdom, is also a symbol of her (snakes are sometimes regarded as sacred animals). The olive is also a symbol (sacred plant) of the goddess, Athena. She

Athena

is the guardian of the city, and for Athena, fighting is to protect the autonomy and peace of the city, unlike Ares (the son of Zeus and Hera) the god of war and courage, who likes to kill each other and thinks that violence takes precedence over anything else. Her temple on the Acropolis, a small hill that symbolized the city, was called the Parthenon.

One day, when Athena visited Hephaestus to make a weapon, the lustful Hephaestus, who was fascinated by Athena's beauty, attacked her, but he failed because Athena resisted with a weapon. The body fluids (semen) of Hephaestus fell to the ground, and from the soil Erichthonius was born as a serpent-formed child. Athena raised Erichthonius in secret, and Erichthonius later became a respected king of Athens.

Another day, when Athena was bathing, Tiresias saw her naked. Athena punished Tiresias and blinded him. However, when Tiresias's mother, Chariclo, begged Athena to heal his son's eyes to be able to see again, Athena gave him the ability to predict the future instead.

Venus

During the Trojan War, Aphrodite (goddess of love, beauty, lust, and pleasure, or supreme beauty, Venus in English) sided with Troy, and Athena and Hera (Zeus's sister and wife, the queen of the gods, and goddess of marriage) sided with Greece. Athena and Hera were both riding on a chariot and going to the battlefield, helping Achilles on the Greek side. The "Trojan Wooden Horse" was taken by the Trojan army as an offering made by the Greeks to calm the anger of Athena, and the huge wooden horse was wrongly brought into the Trojan city. In the end, Troy fell.

## Heracles

Heracles is the greatest hero of Greek mythology. He was a demigod and later became one of the gods of Olympus. His popularity was so great that many royal families in various parts of the Mediterranean claimed that they were descendants of Heracles. In Roman mythology, he is called "Hercules." He is the son of Zeus and the human Alcmene. The word "Hera" in the name of **Hera**cles came from Hera (the jealous wife of Zeus). Zeus wanted to give the power of immortality to the newborn baby Heracles, so he tried to make Heracles suck the milk of his sleeping wife Hera. But Hera was startled awake and pushed the baby away by the intense pain of Heracles' sucking. At that time, the milk that splattered from Hera's breast became the Milky Way (or Galaxy). Alcmene, fearing the wrath of Hera, abandoned the baby (Heracles) in the field, but Athena, on Zeus' orders, picked up the baby and forced Hera to breastfeed. When Hera learned that the baby was Heracules, she hated the baby and released two poisonous snakes into the cradle, but Heracles grabbed the snakes with both hands and killed them. Eventually, Heracles became a brave young warrior who slew a lion at the age of 18. He married Megara and had three children. But one day, at the instigation of Hera, Heracles killed his own

Heracles

children. Returning to sanity, Heracles became aware of the sin he had committed. He asked the Oracle at Delphi to atone for his sin, and as a result, he served King Eurystheus (the great-grandson of Zeus) and obeyed his commands.

Eurystheus ordered Heracules to do 12 difficult tasks. And Heracules had to spend 12 years accomplishing them. The first was the killing of the immortal lion of Nemea. This lion had a tough skin that could not be penetrated by knives. Heracles drove the lion into a cave, blocked the entrance with a large rock, and after three days and three nights of wrestling, strangled it to death. Ever since then, Heracles wore the lion's head and fur and used them as a helmet and armor to fight. This slain lion later became the constellation "Leo." The second challenge was slaying the nine-headed water serpent called Hydra. The monster lived in the lake of Lerna. It had a deadly poison that would kill anyone even if touching it. Heracles struggled with the Hydra that spat out the poison, but he could get rid of it by burying the last remaining immortal head under a rock. Hydra later became the constellation "Sea Snake." Also in this battle, Hera sent a huge crab, which was also defeated and became the constellation "Crab." The third trial was the capture of the sacred hind (deer) offered to Artemis. He had to catch the golden deer without killing it. He finally captured it after a year of chasing, and presented the hind alive to King Eurystheus. The fourth task was to capture of a man-eating boar (Erymanthian boar) that lived on Mount Erymanthus. At this time, Heracles accidentally shot a poisoned arrow of the Hydra at his martial arts teacher, Chiron. Because he could not bear the pain of the poison, Chiron chose to die. Zeus, who regretted the death of Chiron, made him the constellation "Sagittarius." The fifth task was to clean in one day the Augean stables. Augeas, who was king of Elis, raised 3,000 cattle and had not cleaned it for 30 years. The sixth was the extermination of monster birds on the shores of Lake Stymphalia (strangled one by one). The seventh was the capture of a ferocious bull alive in Crete. The eighth was the capture alive of the man-eating horses of King Diomedes. The ninth was to obtain the girdle (waistband) of Hippolyta, Queen of the Amazons. The tenth labor was to bring back the cattle from an island in the far west of the world. The eleventh labor was to steal the sacred fruits (golden apples) protected by Hera. And the last labor (the twelfth) was to bring Cerberus, the three-headed guard dog of the underworld (which was called "the guard dog of hell"), to the earth. Heracles succeeded all the labors and King Eurystheus became wary of the hero's abilities, fearing his power and popularity.

Heracles, who fulfilled these labors with difficulty, went on various adventures and expeditions, and gained a lot of fame. However, in the end, he suffered from the poison caused by his wife's wrong act out of love, ordered himself to be burned to death, and lost his life. At that time, Zeus lifted Heracles up to heaven. With Hera's permission, Heracles was added to the line of gods of Olympus.

## Pandora

Angry that Prometheus, one of the Titans, had stolen fire from the Olympian gods to give it to humans in the form of technology, Zeus created a "human woman" to bring disaster to mankind. Zeus made her shape from mud, and each god sent her every gift. Athena gave her weaving skills and other abilities that a woman should have, Aphrodite gave her a charm that would torment a man, Hermes gave her a shameless and cunning mind, and finally all the gods of Olympus gave her a "box" (originally a jar) that she should never open. Prometheus' younger brother was ecstatic when he saw the beautiful Pandora, broke his brother's advice not to accept any gift from Zeus, and took Pandora as his wife. One day, Pandora became obsessed with the "box" out of curiosity and opened it. Then various plagues, grief, scarcity, crime, etc. flew out of it, and in the end, only "hope" remained. Pandora, at that moment, closed the box. Pandora subsequently survived the Great Flood and became the ancestor of the Greeks. It has been interpreted that humanity can live without despair because "hope" appeared at the end, but there is also an ironic view that hope cannot perform functions if it does not go out of the box and remains closed.

Pandora

Prometheus

"Open Pandora's Box" is now used to mean "to create an opportunity to invite disaster," but since "hope" remains in it, it can also mean that those who are in a difficult situation should expect to be reborn, not give up hope, and take on new challenges. If we go back to the beginning, this story should be interpreted as follows: As the result of deceiving Zeus and stealing fire for the sake of mankind, humans were forced to live a life of suffering and calamity at the cost of using fire.

## Odysseus

Odysseus is one of the heroes of Greek mythology, and he is the protagonist of Homer's epic poem *Odysseia*. In Latin, Odysseus is called "Ulixes," and in English, it is called "Ulysses."

Odysseus, king of Ithaca, took part in the siege of Troy. While the other warriors were fierce attackers, Odysseus was a wise general who fought with his knowledge. He was a hero who was also favored by the goddess Athena. It was Odysseus who kept fighting after Achilles' death and devised the "Trojan Horse" operation that would end the nine-year war. The trick succeeded when Odysseus and other brave warriors were lurking in the huge wooden horse, and inducing the enemy soldiers to carry the wooden horse into the walled-city. In addition, Poseidon sent giant serpents to kill the enemy Laocoön (a Trojan priest) and his two young sons, who were suspicious of the wooden horse. In the evening, the Trojans celebrated their victory and held a banquet, got drunk,

Trojan Horse

and fell asleep. Then Odysseus and others came out of the wooden horse and signaled to the Greeks with torches, drawing them into the city and killed the enemies, including the Trojan king. This bizarre tactic, devised and practiced by Odysseus, led to the fall of the city of Troy.

Odysseus then set sail for his homeland, but it was a long and painful journey that lasted more than ten years, longer than the Trojan War. Meanwhile, his son Telemachus embarked on an adventurous journey to find his father. Odysseus finally returned to his homeland after a difficult time, only to find that people living there believed he was already dead, and his territory was ransacked. His wife, Queen Penelope was courted by 40 men in order to inherit her inheritance. Odysseus swept them away with his son and his servants. Finally, Odysseus lived in peace with his beloved Penelope and son Telemachus. The suitors' relatives tried to get revenge, but Athena stopped them.

James Joyce (1882-1941) born and educated in Ireland, was the greatest novelist in the 20th century English literature. He became famous for using a new writing style, known as "a stream of consciousness," which greatly influenced the later writers. *Dubliners* (1914), *A Portrait of an Artist as a Young Man* (1916), *Ulysses* (1922), and *Finnegan's Wake* (1939) are his masterpieces. The

Odysseus

novel title *Ulysses* is the English version of *Ulixes*, dealing with a Greek mythological hero, Odysseus, and consisting of more than 680 pages in paperback. The novel written by Joyce is a work composed of 18 episodes that depict the undistinguished events of a day in Dublin, Ireland, and are full of thoughts and feelings of the ordinary characters. However, they are representatives of heroes in Homer's epic, *Odysseia* in the 8th century BC, and it links them to cross ancient and modern history. The daily life of middle-aged, unpopular Dubliners is depicted using esoteric terms, and sometimes the characters' monologues continue endlessly.

Leopold Bloom, a dull, middle-aged man, is Odysseus, his son Stephen Dedalus, an aspiring writer, is Telemachus, and his unfaithful wife, Molly Bloom, is likened to the chaste queen Penelope. Twenty years of suffering have been replaced by a single day on 16 June 1904.

The main settings of the story are as follows: the parapet of the tower, school, Sandymount Strand, Eccles Street, All Hallows (church), Westland Row, a pharmacy, the mosque of the baths, Prospects (graveyard), a lane of sepulchers, the Press, the national library, the Ormond (hotel) bar, Barney Kiernan's (inn), hospital, whore town, the cabman's shelter (tearoom), and the bedroom. In the ninth episode, the philosophers Plato, Aristotle, and later Socrates appeared, and Shakespeare is called "Saxon Shakespeare," then the author introduces the theory that Shakespeare had a son named "Hamnet Shakespeare" who died at the age of 20. *Hamlet* is said to be a tragic work created in the image of his dead son. His masterpiece was greatly influenced by his own life. There are various words in the text: musical terms such as piano, diminuendo, a tempo, stringendo; Latin, Italian, French, German, Gaelic; frequently quotes from Shakespeare plays and sonnets. In the fourteenth episode, there are many topics about obstetrics, gynecology, mother's womb, pregnancy, fetus, and childbirth, expressed in various writing ways using old English-style, Middle English-style, Latin, Irish, etc. The final eighteenth episode is tremendous; its original title was "Penelope," the name of Odyssey's chaste wife. The content of the text is only the image of the cheating wife of Leopold Bloom in bed. It is exclusively her inner monologue, in other words, "the stream of consciousness" that covers more than 40 pages without apostrophes or commas, and almost no punctuation marks. It should be noted that in the distant past, the person who should be the main character of the story was God, the royalty and aristocracy, the hero, the great man, and the ideal person. More than 2,000 years later, they became strange literary young men or ordinary middle-aged people who could not be models, and who could not be the main characters of the story before. A mixture of traditional Catholic worldviews and metaphors of obscene sexual depictions is also a feature of this work. The experimental novel was published in Paris in 1922. It was four years after the end of the First World War (1914-18), by which more than 16 million people were killed. This chaotic and avant-garde novel ends with the word, "Yes." This is indeed symbolic and it is a sign of Joyce's hope for the future of humanity. This literary work is undoubtedly one of the goals of world literature in the 20$^{th}$ century.

## Apollo

Apollo was the son of Zeus, the god of the arts, the god of bows and arrows, and in Roman times he became the god of the sun. Apollo's sacred

Apollo 1

beasts are wolves, serpents, and deer. His sacred birds are swans, roosters, hawks, etc., and his sacred trees are laurels, olives, etc. When his jealous wife, Hera, learned that Zeus and another woman (Leto) were about to give birth to the glorious Apollo, Hera prohibited the nations of the world from providing a place for childbirth. As a result, when Leto gave birth to Apollo, she suffered the pain of a desperate birth.

Hyacinthus was a human boy in Greek mythology. He was not only a famous beautiful boy in Greece, but also an athletic athlete who was loved by everyone who knew him. Apollo met him in the arena, and Apollo taught him music and poetry, and eventually they fell in love. One day, however, he was playing a game of discus with Apollo, and the disc that Apollo threw hit him in the head, killing him. Apollo mourned his death and turned his corpse into a flower (or the blood flowing from his forehead turned into a flower). This flower is called hyacinth. Another theory is that this flower is not the current hyacinth but the current iris, or pansy. Apollo is said to have composed many poems and music that reminded him of Hyacinthus.

Orpheus, the son of Apollo, was skilled in the lyre (harp) and singing, and when he sang, not only the birds and beasts of the forest but even the trees and stones began to dance with joy. He took a fairy as his wife, but shortly after their marriage, she died from the bite of a poisonous snake lurking in the grass.

There is also a story of the maiden (Sibyl) who rejected Apollo's love. Apollo told her that he would grant her any wish as a token of his love. Then she grabbed the sand with one hand and said that she wanted as many lives as this number of grains of sand. While receiving the gift, she rejected Apollo's love. Eventually, Apollo forgot her. She gained a thousand-year lifespan, but she was struck by old age and felt despaired. When the children asked, "Sibyl, what do you want? Do you want anything?" she replied, "I want death." How much she regretted that she did not say that she wished not only longevity but also imperishable youth.

Apollo, who was skilled in music and the arts, also gave the Greeks the maxims such as "Do not overdo it." and "Know thyself." It is said that Greek philosophy developed from this second maxim.

John Keats (1795-1821) was born in London, England. Many of Keats' poems deal with the theme of beauty, and he is described as a "martyr of beauty." He often sought Greek mythology as a subject, leaving these words, "A thing of beauty is a joy forever," "What is more gentle than a wind in summer?", and "Beauty is truth, truth beauty." Keats died of tuberculosis in Rome, Italy, at the age of 25. *Endymion*, who seeks eternal beauty, is his masterpiece.

DEEP in the shady sadness of vale
Far sunken from the healthy breath of morn,
Far from the fiery noon, and eve's one star,
Sat gray-hair'd Saturn, quiet as a stone,

Still as the silence round about his lair;

Forest on forest hung about his head

Like cloud on cloud. No stir of air was there,

Not so much life as on a summer's day

Robs not one light seed from the feather'd grass,

But where the dead leaf fell, there did it rest.

A stream went voiceless by, still deadened more

By reason of his fallen divinity

Spreading a shade: the Naiad 'mid her reeds

Press'd her cold finger closer to her lips

Hyperion — A Fragment Book 1[1]


But eagles golden-feather'd, who do tower

Above us in their beauty, and must reign

In right thereof; for 'tis the eternal law

That first in beauty should be first in might;

Hyperion — A Fragment Book II[2]


And I was stopped up my frantic ears,

When, past all hindrance of my trembling hands,

A voice came, sweeter, sweeter than all tune,

And still it cried, "Apollo! young Apollo!"

Hyperion — A Fragment Book II[3]


'Hyperion' is a work that deals with Greek mythology like Keat's previous work, the narrative poem *Endymion* (1817). 'Hyperion' is also an epic poem that he began to work on after the completion of his previous work. It depicts the conflict between the old and new gods, and at the same time it depicts the historical turning point in England and Europe in the early

Apollo 2

19th century, but it was unfinished. Hyperion in Greek Mythology was the god who represented the old system, and the god of the new age was represented by Apollo.

# 4. Socrates: The Man Who Loved Dialogue

## Greek philosophy

In explaining or thinking about something, a person must discern what the essence of the thing is, or he must know what is at the root of the world. The Old Testament, the holy book of Christianity, begins with God's creation of the heavens and the earth. It describes the origin of the universe in which we humans are. And God, who is the source of all things, gives meaning to everything in this world. Why do birds fly in the sky, fish swim in rivers, and horses run on the earth? Why does the sun rise during the day and the stars shine at night? Why do we get hungry and sleepy? What are you, what were you born for, and what is the right way to live? The Bible tells us that the answers to these questions are in God. But this cannot be called philosophy.

Thales

This is because they have not confirmed the existence of God for themselves and have just accepted the contents of the Bible as it is. They can believe teachings of religion, but cannot know objective evidence. If you think logically, philosophy is about exploring the rules of the world that everyone can agree on. Thales (620-540s BC), the founder of Greek philosophy, said, "The source of all things is water." The principle of all things in the world is water. This is the trigger for many people to start thinking logically about how this world works. Thales made a great leap from mythology to logic (logos). He was a native of Miletus, an ancient Greek city in the Ionian region of Asia Minor (present-day Turkey) on the Aegean Sea. Thales, who was a mathematician, predicted eclipses and calculated the height of the pyramids of Egypt from his height. Homer, the 8th-century BC Ancient Greek poet, famous as the author of the *Iliad* and the *Odyssey*, is also said to have been from Ionia. Pythagoras (582-496 BC) was born

Hippocrates

the son of a lapidary on the island of Samos in the Ionian region. Hippocrates (460-370s BC), one of the greatest Greek physicians of Socrates' time, was also born on the island of Kos, near the Ionian region. Hippocrates, the Father of Medicine, is said to have been born into a family of medical scientists whose ancestor was Asclepius (the son of Apollo and Coronis), a hero (demigod), and a god of medicine. Hippocrates believed that illness was a natural occurrence and not the work of supernatural superstition, witchcraft, evil spirits, or gods. Ionia was located just across the Aegean Sea from Athens. Like Athens, it seems to have been an important commercial city in ancient Greece. A wide variety of goods from the countries along the Mediterranean coast were distributed, and at the same time, various information and values flowed in, and it must have been full of things that stimulated intellectual curiosity. There is no doubt that the fact that they were financially well-off gave people a sense of mental space and encouraged their interest in rational ways of thinking and philosophical ideas.

Pythagoras

Soon in Greece, philosophy was the basis of all learning. Pythagoras, who is now famous as a mathematician, was a philosopher. In the 21$^{st}$ century era, a medical doctor still hopes to become a philosophy doctor (Ph.D.). Both the humanities and sciences are eventually in the category of philosophy. In studying European literature, it is impossible to properly understand the author's message without a deep understanding of Christian doctrine. Similarly, without keeping a grasp of the history of Western philosophy, we cannot understand European literature. In particular, contemporary literature cannot be discussed without Nietzsche or Sartre, and the same is true for structuralism and post-structuralism. Philosophy is the basis of all kinds of study. And the philosophy originated in ancient Greece.

In 507 BC, democracy was introduced to Athens for the first time in the world. As a result, most of the people (except women, children, and slaves) were able to participate in politics. So, those who wanted to succeed politically had to learn how to speak persuasively. Then, the profession of teaching the art of eloquence arose, and the sophists appeared. The word "sophist" meant "wise man." They traveled all over the Mediterranean, learned many things, and came to Athens as wise men to receive money and instruct the citizens. However, since their sole purpose was to teach how to win the controversy and to earn money, there were a lot of quibbles. Before long, the word "sophist" came to be used to mean "sophistries." Then Socrates (470-399 BC) appeared. He was born in Athens, as the son of a stonemason (also a sculptor). His mother was a midwife. As a young man, Socrates went to one of the colonies of Athens, serving as an infantryman to suppress a rebellion, but he spent most of his life in Athens.

One day, one of his friends went to the Temple of Apollo at Delphi and heard, "There is no one wiser than Socrates in the world." Socrates thought he knew nothing about this world, so he decided to have a dialogue with the statemen and poets (artists) who were called wise men at the time to see if the divine message was really correct. And when Socrates asked many questions about their thoughts and theories, he realized that none of the wise men could answer. They had no understanding of the essence of beauty, goodness, and other things that were most important to human beings. Socrates realized that those who called themselves wise men were not aware that they knew nothing about the world. He also realized he was wiser than they were because he, himself, was aware he knew nothing about the world.

When people mistake themselves for being omniscient, they don't try to know anything more. Socrates realized that we should be aware that we know nothing about. If we assume we know everything, we will be satisfied with the current situation and will not try to find something new. However, if we realize that we are ignorant, we will be motivated to pursue the truth voraciously. It is also the idea of knowing one's true self by becoming aware of ignorance. The proverb "Know thyself," inscribed on the pillar of the Temple of Apollo, was the starting point of philosophy for Socrates. In this sense, he was also

Socrates

a conservative philosopher.

We sometimes feel that we have seen and heard everything and know everything, but that is only how we interpret what we see and hear, and in fact, we do not understand what the essence of everything is. No one knows, but God. However, only the genuine "worldview" that unfolds in one's own mind that interprets something is undoubtedly the truth that the person has. I wonder if Socrates, with his "knowledge of ignorance," tried to reset the pedantic worldview, and also tried to start a genuine philosophy of knowing what the real self is (Socrates himself did not make such a statement about the "knowledge of ignorance," and in fact the philosopher known for initiating a philosophy of searching for his own truth was Kierkegaard). That is why Socrates has an unwavering presence in the history of philosophy. Also, he insisted that everyone tries to live righteously, but sometimes they go astray and fall into evil because they do not know what is good and what is bad. Evil deeds come from ignorance of goodness. Socrates

The Death of Socrates

taught everyone that by knowing virtue, one can live a good life. *Arete* (virtue) was the most important concept of Socrates in his later years. He also said that those who live by practicing virtue and goodness are happy.

Socrates understood that Apollo had set himself on a mission to make people aware of their ignorance, and he did his utmost to refute and persuade many sophists and his fellow citizens of Athens to realize they were ignorant. But while his activities produced supporters around him, many influential people and their colleagues who were dragged into debate and subjected to their ignorance felt resentment against Socrates and grew to hate him. Some young men appeared to imitate Socrates' examination, and that made senior citizens angry. As a result, Socrates was accused of corrupting youth and sentenced to death. He drank poison and died at the age of 71. For Socrates, however, death was by no means a pessimistic ending. After his death sentence, he told a friend who had come to see him and tried to encourage Socrates to go into exile, that the important thing was "not just to live, but to live as a person of high virtue." He valued dialogue and left nothing written.

# 5. **Plato:** The Theory of Ideas

Plato

Plato was born in Athens, ancient Greece, in 427 BC. He is said to come from a prestigious family with royal blood. When he was young, Plato was strong in wrestling with a good physique. He was skilled in both literary and martial arts. He aspired to be a politician, but at the age of 28, he witnessed the arrest and death penalty of his mentor Socrates, who died of a poisoned chalice. Plato decided to choose the path of pursuing the truth of man.

Plato was the author of *Apology of Socrates*, *Phaedo*, *The Republic*, and so on. He was a disciple of Socrates and advocated the Theory of Ideas (=Theory of Forms). In other words, "Idea" from the theory is the idea that there is a real, ideal, and perfect form, and that the world we live in now is only a shadow of the ideal world and it is imperfect. He emphasized mathematics and geometry, and used them as the basis for supporting his "Theory of Ideas" as a true reality beyond human senses.

Plato wrote many plays called "Platonic Dialogues" over a period of half a century, from his thirties to the age of eighty. Many of his writings feature his mentor, Socrates, as the main character, and the story consists of conversations between Socrates and other characters. *Phaedo* is one of the series of the Dialogues, in which Plato's unique philosophy, "Theory of Ideas," appears for the first time. *Phaedo* depicts the day of Socrates' execution through dialogue, and on the morning of his execution, Socrates, who is allowed to see and converse with his friends, enjoys a lively dialogue. Socrates speaks of the relationship between body and soul, arguing that for philosophers, death is never an abomination nor calamity but rather the final liberation of the soul imprisoned in the body. Then, in the evening, Socrates drank poison and died. In this story, the concept of the eternal and unchanging Idea is presented as an argument for the proof of the immortality of the soul. The Idea world is the perfect one of eternal immortality. The Idea world is real, and the earth on which we live is like a shadow of the Idea, and man is the form of the soul that has fallen from the Idea world and combined with the body. We see, hear, and touch things in the world in which we live, and perceive them with our senses, but they are imperfect beings that imitate Ideas. Ideas, which exist truly, do not rely on the senses, but rely on reason. We can recognize Ideas if we think logically in our heads, and correctly discern between truth and falsehood, or good and evil. They can be recognized by such a power of reason.

Plato explains the metaphor of the cave in his work, *The Republic*. A prisoner trapped in a dark cave sees a shadow cast on a wall by the light of a torch. He thinks it is a true reality. If he sees a dog's shadow, he thinks it's a real dog, and if he sees a crab's shadow, he recognizes it as a real crab. To study philosophy is to come out of a cave and see the outside world where the sun shines. It is a very easy example to understand, but it can also be thought of in a way that is more familiar to us. To paraphrase the cave metaphor in a modern way, it is a person who is trapped in a virtual space. Plato's argument is just like saying that the world that everyone thinks is real is a virtual space.

If all the information we get through our five senses is created by computers, we cannot believe what we see. Since the truth that philosophers should seek is in the real world (the world of Ideas) that creates the virtual space, they should use reason instead of relying on sensibility. However, while it is fun to fantasize about the story that this reality is a virtual space, many people will feel that they cannot understand the spirit of serious attempts to try to figure it out as a scholar. In *Phaedo*, Plato gives evidence for the existence of Ideas. In *Phaedo*, Plato cites the basis on which the Idea exists. For example, there are concepts that are "beautiful" or "right" and it is difficult to clearly define what they refer to. All of this has an answer to the Idea. The human soul is originally in the world of Ideas, and because we are born into this world, the soul is imprisoned in the body. However, the reason why we think something is "right" and feel something is "beautiful," is because we remember the "right"

The School of Athens

and "beautiful" that our soul knew when it lived in the Idea world. This is called "anamnēsis (recollection theory)."

It is worth noting that Plato's Theory of Ideas not only had a great influence on later philosophers but also became an important source of the Romantic view of art in the 19th century. Plato also developed a theory of the state, talking about what the state is and what justice is. He envisioned an ideal state ruled by philosophers trained to realize the Idea of goodness in the world.

At the age of 39, he left Athens and visited Egypt, Italy, and the island of Sicilia (Sikelia). After the age of 40, Plato founded a school in Akadēmeíā (Academia) on the outskirts of Athens, where he taught astronomy, biology, mathematics, political science, geometry, and philosophy. He raised many disciples. The educational goal was to direct the soul of youth from this world to the world of Ideas, and when Plato was 60 years old, Aristotle (17 years old), appeared among those disciples. There is a masterpiece called *The School of Athens* (*Scuola di Atene*: 1510), painted by Raffaello Sanzi (1483-1520), an Italian painter of the Renaissance period. It is symbolic that Plato in the painting points with his right hand to the heavens (which evokes the world of Ideas), and Aristotle indicates his right hand toward the ground (which emphasizes the exploration of the real world). Plato died at the age of 80, in 347 BC.

# 6. Aristotle: Erudite Person

Aristotle

The ancient Greek philosopher, Aristotle, was born in 384 BC in the ancient Kingdom of Macedonia. He was the son of a physician who served Amyntas III, the king of Macedonia, who was the grandfather of Alexander the Great (356-323 BC). Like Hippocrates, his family was thought to be related to Asclepius, the god of medicine. He lost both his parents at an early age. At the age of 17, he came to Athens to enter Academia and started studying under Plato for about 20 years. After Plato's death, he returned to Macedonia, and at the age of 42, he became a tutor for Alexander the Great, who was then 13 years old. At the age of 49, with the accession of Alexander to the throne, he returned to Athens and founded a school in Lyceum (Lykeion), a suburb of Athens. While Plato's Academy was devoted to abstract speculation, Aristotle's Lyceum focused on scientific studies. Aristotle wrote *Organum*, *Physics*, *Metaphysics*, *Politics*, and many more. In fact, most of the works attributed to Aristotle were compilations of his lecture notes.

Aristotle studied and classified every discipline: logic, biology, physics, astronomy, meteorology, zoology, botany, psychology, literature, aesthetics, political science, economics, ethics, metaphysics, etc. Because he laid the foundation for those disciplines, he is regarded as the father of all kinds of learning. He also rejected his mentor Plato's Theory of Ideas, and advocated the philosophy of realism. He defined Plato's way of thinking idealism. According to the Theory of Ideas, Idea, the essence of everything in the world and the norm of everything should be pursued as an ideal form. However, Aristotle insists on the opposite position that values the reality present here on earth rather than aiming for the ideal. Aristotle's realism is the idea that truth exists in the real world in which we live, and that the essence of everything is in the thing itself. He called the essence inherent in everything "eidos (form)," and called the material or substance of eidos "hyle."

Thus, Aristotle's ideas are often at odds with his mentor Plato. For example, when asked what "courage" is, Plato replied that there is an Idea of "courage" and that the closer you get to the ideal, the more desirable it is. But Aristotle replied that since it is not good for any emotion to be extreme, "courage" should be somewhere between recklessness and cowardice. It is best to be moderate. The reason why the ideas of the two philosophers are at odds is that Plato's philosophy was similar to mysticism, as can be seen from the fact that it later had a great influence on theology, whereas Aristotle was a philosopher who made many achievements in the field of natural science.

Aristotle replied to the question "What do people live for?" by saying, "The ultimate goal of mankind is happiness." He said that true happiness required a long life and that it is important to acquire "virtue" in order to be happy. "Virtue" he said, is "courage," "temperance," "fraternity," "justice," "pride," and "moderation." He also emphasized the importance of "friendship." He asserted, "Without friends, no one would want to live, even if he had all other goods."

Aristotle's scholarship contributed greatly to the later advancement of science, but he was particularly interested in flora and fauna. Since he was once a tutor to Alexander the Great, he is said to have asked the Great King to send samples of the local flora and fauna of the conquered lands. Aristotle was also interested in astronomy. Plato said that since the divine maker of the earth is perfect, the earth created must also be perfect, and he said that the earth is round from the idea that the circle is a perfect shape. The people of ancient Greece generally believed that the earth was flat. Aristotle, however, observed the phases of the moon, and although he argued for the Ptolemaic theory, Aristotle insisted that the earth was round, by analogy from the shadows of the earth's curves projected on the moon. This episode illustrates well the characteristics of the two geniuses, Plato and Aristotle. And, of course, Aristotle's ideas led to later empiricism. In his later years, Aristotle spent his time in his mother's hometown, Chalcis, ancient Greek. He died there in 322 BC, at the age of 62.

# 7. Roman Empire

It was Rome that adopted and developed the culture of Greece. The city-state of Rome eventually became a monarchy (for 244 years). Then in 509 BC, the Romans expelled the last king from the city and

Julius Caesar (right side)

established the Roman Republic (Res Publica Romana), which afterwards unified the peninsula of Italy (272 BC). The Roman Republic further expanded its territory through wars, and the areas conquered by Rome (later the Roman Empire) outside of the Italian peninsula were called Roman provinces, and taxes were collected from them. Each province was ruled by a Roman governor (or a military commander). After the First Triumvirate of Pompey, Crassus, and Julius Caesar (100-44 BC), Rome became a dictatorship under Caesar (49 BC). On 15 March 44 BC, Caesar was assassinated by Brutus and Cassius. This was followed by the Second Triumvirate between Antony (Caesar's relative), Lepidus, and Octavian (Caesar's great-nephew, later Caesar's adopted son and heir). Each of them confronted and fought, and Lepidus was exiled in 36 BC. After Octavian's victory against Antony and Cleopatra at the Battle of Actium in 31 BC, Octavian (=Caesar Augustus) changed the form of government from a republic to an empire.

Emperor Hadrianus

After Octavian's death, his adopted son Tiberius became emperor. After that, during the reign of so-called "Five Good Emperors" including Emperor Hadrianus (76-138 AD), the Roman Empire was the most prosperous and the most stable (96-180 AD).

Even today, if you visit Rome, you will find many ruins from the Roman Empire that are of high cultural value. First of all, there is the Colosseum, which is a tourist destination that represents Rome, the capital of Italy, and is said to be a symbol of ancient Rome. This amphitheater was first built by Emperor Vespasianus (9-79 AD) in 70 AD and was completed by the emperor's son Titus in 80 AD. The ruins of Mercatus Traiani, an ancient Roman shopping mall, remain in the middle of Rome. The market was founded between 100 and 110 by Emperor Trajanus (53-117

Colosseum

AD). The Aurelian Wall (Mura aureliane) was built in the $3^{rd}$ century with a total length of 19 kilometers to expand the old city wall built in the $4^{th}$ century BC. The Roman Emperor Aurelianus (214-

275) ordered its construction in 270 and completed it five years later, but the emperor died before it was completed. Castel Sant'Angelo, a round castle, was completed in 139 by Hadrianus'

Mercatus Traiani

order as his own mausoleum. In 403, it was incorporated into part of the Aurelian Wall. The castle had a military significance and was fully fortified in the 14th century. 700 meters west of the castle is la Basilica di San Pietro, the headquarters of the Catholic Church. It is located in the southeast of the Vatican City State. It is said that the tomb of the martyr Peter was originally located there, and was

built by Constantinus I as a church to commemorate the martyr, Peter (Pietro). The Fontana di Trevi is the largest man-made fountain in Rome. Originally built by Emperor Augustus (Caesar's

Aurelian Wall

Castel Sant'Angelo

adopted son), it was completed in 1762 at the behest of Pope Clemens XII (1652-1740). Villa Adriana (Tivoli) is a villa built by Emperor Hadrianus between 118 and 133 AD in a place 30 km east of Rome.

The Roman Empire ruled over all the countries facing the Mediterranean (Greece, Turkey, Syria, Egypt, northern Africa, Spain, Portugal, etc.), and its rule extended to present- day France, England, Wales, Belgium, Netherlands and Germany. A representative of the ruins of the Roman provinces in Europe is maybe Pont du Gard (Roman Aqueduct) in the south of France. This 53-kilometer-long archaeological site is the best-preserved Roman aqueduct. It was probably built around the $1^{st}$ century AD, perhaps between 40 and 50 AD. Other important Roman ruins in Europe are, for example, Hadrian's Wall in Britain, the Roman defensive fortification to separate England and

Basilica di San Pietro

Scotland, begun to be built in 122 AD in the reign of the Emperor Hadrianus. The Roman Baths (built in the $1^{st}$ century) in the city of Bath, England, are also well-preserved Roman ruins in

Britain. In Germany, the Porta Nigra (built in 200 AD) is very popular. It was a large Roman city gate built in gray sandstone with two four-story towers.

Fontana di Trevi

Next, we must see the relationship between the Roman Empire and Christianity. This is because Christianity, which would mentally support and nurture European civilization, was born during the Roman Empire. Christianity was first persecuted by the Roman Empire and eventually became the Roman Empire's state religion.

After the execution of Jesus Christ, the Roman Empire allowed the province of Judea to be self-governed at first, but as the Jews repeatedly rebelled against tax payments and conscription, they eventually switched to the direct rule, including the destruction of the holy temple in Jerusalem. Christians were also expelled from Judaism and persecuted by the Roman Empire. However, Christianity eventually spread to all corners of the Roman Empire through Peter, a direct disciple of Jesus, and Paul, who was

Villa Adriana

Hadrian's Wall

born in Tarsus in Asia Minor and had Roman citizenship, who emphasized evangelism to the Gentiles. Paul was initially on the side of persecuting Christians, but after an "eye-opening" experience, he became an apostle. Finally, he was beheaded by Emperor Nero. It is said that it's to Paul's achievements that Christianity became a universal world religion rather than a reformed form of Judaism. Paul declared, "Man is not saved by keeping the law of God, but only by believing in the love of Jesus Christ."

Constantine the Great (272-337) was the first Roman emperor to become a Christian. He reunited the empire, which was in a state of chaos at that time due to the scattering of emperors in various places, under the protection of Christianity. As a result, he became the first emperor to protect the Christian religion, which had been persecuted before. In 313, he made Christianity an official religion (although it was one of many recognized religions). When Emperor Constantine moved the capital of the Roman Empire to Constantinople

Pont du Gard

(before Byzantium, now Istanbul) in 330, the City of Rome became the capital of the Pope and the Church of Rome. In 392, Emperor Theodosius (347-395) made Christianity the Roman Empire's state religion. It seems that the emperor tried to use Christianity to rule the empire, because Christianity had a strong sense of unity, a large number of followers, and an ever-increasing number of Christians. And the Christian doctrine came to be interpreted in the convenience of the emperor (for example, the emperor is God's agent to have the divine right to reign over the people). Upon his death,

Porta Nigra

Emperor Theodosius nominated his two sons as Western and Eastern Roman Emperors, respectively. Then, the East-West split of the Roman Empire became decisive. In other words, it was the start of the division of the church into the Eastern Orthodox and Roman Catholic ones.

Later, the Roman Catholic Church (Western Roman Empire) sided with the Germanic tribes, and when the kingdom of Franks (present-day Germany, France, and Italy) established itself at the end of the $5^{th}$ century (454), the pope asked the Frankish king to donate some territory to him. So, the pope himself became a feudal lord. After all, the Western Roman Empire was destroyed by the Germanic Roman General Odoacer in 476. Islam (founded by Muhammad), which originated in the Arabian Peninsula in the $7^{th}$ century, quickly spread to Syria, Palestine, Persia, and North Africa, and antagonized Christian countries in northwestern Europe (Latin, Germanic, and Celtic ones). The Eastern Roman Empire fell in 1453. The Muslim world expanded its power and oppressed Christian countries. But in the $16^{th}$ century, the Renaissance took place in the West, and the balance of power changed. Thereafter, Western Christian nations gained the upper hand.

# 8. Christianity

Jesus Christ

It is said that the Jewish people were formed between 2,100 BC and 1,500 BC, and the Old Testament had been written for about 1,000 years and is still the only canon of Judaism. In Christianity, the Old Testament is canonical along with the New Testament. In Islam, which also arose in the Middle East (in the $7^{th}$ century), both the Old Testament and the New Testament are considered to be scriptures or documents that record divine revelation (prophecy), but the Qur'an (Koran) takes precedence. The Old Testament, which consists of 39 books beginning with the Book of Genesis, was originally written in Hebrew, but was translated into Greek in the $3^{rd}$ century BC.

The New Testament is the promise of new salvation of the Messiah Jesus Christ, and consists of 27 books written in Greek, including the life of Jesus Christ, His Resurrection after the Crucifixion, and His teachings. All the contents were written by the disciples after Jesus' death. Christianity originated in Israel in the Middle East, but eventually expanded westward and became a representative religion that supported Western civilization or European society, and still has more than 2.3 billion followers in the world. One-third of the world's population is Christian (Muslims are about the same number, but it is certain to surpass Christians in the near future). Christianity is now divided into three main groups: Catholicism, Protestantism, and the Eastern Orthodox Church.

It should be noted that December 25 was decided to be Christmas in 354 AD, and before that it was presumed to be in January or May. It is also said that Jesus' birthday was actually between 6 and 4 BC (It was in the years 532 AD that people began to be counted the years in the Christian calendar). It is said that the place where Jesus was born is not Bethlehem, but Nazareth. It is also pointed out that "true socialism is the inevitable result of Christianity." For modern rationalists who deny God, the existence of God would be a reflection of human aspirations. According to their view, it is possible to look back on the life of Jesus Christ and evaluate him as a great man, a great philosopher, not associated with religious activities or Christianity, which later became a major religion all over the world.

Today, Christians in the UK are said to be about 60% of the population. However, only about one in ten of them goes to church every week, and at most one in five people goes to church about once a month. Less than 10% of the population follow other religions, including Muslims, Hindus, and Buddhists, and about 25% have no religion. It is also said that young people rarely go to church. Many churches are in danger of closing the church, selling historical buildings, or demolition due to financial difficulties to keep the building. Nonetheless, the coronations of kings and queens, royal weddings, Christmas events, relief efforts for homeless people, and charity events for the poor suggest that Christianity is firmly rooted in British culture and British life. And Christianity is still involved in people's everyday lives, and more connected to citizens than Japanese Buddhism and Shintoism. I think British Christian culture still deeply influences their way of life.

## The Old Testament

### The Creation of the World

In the book of Genesis, God, who created the heavens and the earth, created man in the image of God, saying, "Fill the earth and make the earth subjugate, and rule over all the fish of the sea, the birds of the air, and all the creatures that crawl on the earth."

> In the beginning God created the heaven and the earth.
>
> And the earth was without form, and void; and darkness was upon
>
> The face of the deep.
>
> And the Spirit of God moved upon the face of the waters.
>
> And God said, Let there be light: and there was light.
>
> And God saw the light, that it was good: and God divided the light from the darkness.
>
> And God called the light Day, and the darkness he called Night.
>
> And the evening and the morning were the first day. [4]

*Genesis, Authorized King James Version*

### Adam and Eve

In the center of the Garden of Eden were the Tree of Life and the Tree of Wisdom. God commanded Adam not to eat the fruit of knowledge. Then a woman was created, and a serpent approached her and tempted her to eat the fruit of knowledge, and when she ate the fruit, she invited Adam to eat it, and Adam also ate it. Then, their eyes opened, and they realized that they were naked, and they were ashamed of it, so they covered their waists with fig leaves. As a result, the serpent became a belly-crawling creature, the woman suffered the pain of childbirth, and the man had to work in the sweat of his brow to obtain food. Adam named her Eve. God was

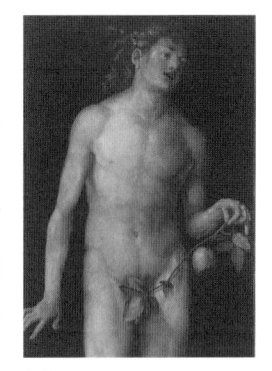
Adam

Eve

afraid that the fruit of the Tree of Life would also be eaten, and banished them from Paradise. From this, man's death became decisive and he lost eternal life.

## Cain and Abel

Cain and Abel were brothers born to Adam and Eve who were driven out of the Garden of Eden. The elderly brother's name is Cain, and the younger brother is Abel. Cain farmed, and Abel grazed sheep. One day, they

Paradise Lost

offered their tributes to God (Jehovah). Cain offered the harvest, and Abel offered the lamb. God took notice of Abel's offering, but not Cain's. Cain, who resented this attitude of God, invited Abel into the field and killed him. Later, God asked Cain where Abel was going, to which Cain replied, "I don't know, because I'm not my brother's keeper." However, Abel's death naturally became known to God, and Cain was banished to the east

Cain and Abel

of Eden. God told him that Cain could no longer harvest even though he cultivates the land, and that God told him that there would be sevenfold revenge on those who kill Cain, so that Cain would not be killed by the people of the land. Cain eventually had a son, Enoch. God also gave Adam and Eve their third son, Seth, to replace Abel. Cain, who killed Abel, became the first human murderer. It is said that Cain's descendants were the targets that were destroyed in the later Great Flood, but on the other hand, God protected Cain even though he committed murder. This would show God's deep love for a human being, not wanting to destroy the man He created in His own image.

## Noah's Ark

When God saw the corruption of the people who had multiplied on the earth, He told Noah (the righteous man) that He would destroy them

Ark (right) and Noah's prayer (left)

by flooding, and He commanded Noah to build an ark. The ark was made of wood and had three floors. When Noah completed the ark, he placed his wife, his three sons, their respective wives, and all the animals on the ark. The flood lasted 40 days, and the water did not lose momentum for 150 days, killing all creatures on the ground. The ark remained on top of the mountain. After several trials and errors, the last pigeon released returned to the ship with an olive leaf. Eventually, the water began to dry up, and Noah and his family left the ark, built an altar there, and made offerings to God. The Lord blessed them and put a rainbow in the sky.

## The Tower of Babel

God gave the descendants of Noah, who survived the Flood, parts of the world and commanded them to live there. The people of all the lands used the same language. As the people gathered, some of the immigrants from the East said, "Come, let's build our city and our tower." They began to build a tall tower that would reach to the heavens. When God saw this, He anticipated the completion of the tower and made the people's language incomprehensible to each other. This caused confusion; people were unable to complete the tower, and building the city was canceled. And the story goes that the people scattered to various places. Is a tall tower a symbol of human pride?

The Tower of Babel

## Abraham and his son Isaac

This is a story that shows the depth of Abraham's fear and faith in God. One of Noah's descendants, Abraham, was already old but he had no children. His wife, Sarai, encouraged him to take a female Egyptian servant, Hagar, as his concubine, and as a result, at the age of 85, he had a son, Ishmael. Abraham, who later turned 100 years old, had a legitimate son, Isaac, with his old wife, Sarah (=Sarai). When Abraham was 137 years old, Abraham and his son Isaac were subjected to a great test of God. In other words, Abraham, who always feared God and was renowned as an exemplary believer, loved his legitimate son Isaac more than anything else, but one day (just before Sarah's death), God commanded him to sacrifice Isaac. Abraham, obedient and devout, got up early in the morning, chopped wood to burn the sacrifice, saddled his donkey, and took two of his followers and Isaac to the summit site (or temple mount) that God had indicated. Carrying firewood on his back and climbing to the top of the mountain, Isaac became confused by the lack of a lamb to offer, but soon realized that he was a sacrifice. Isaac did not resist, but was tied up with a rope and placed on the altar. The moment Abraham raised his knife at Isaac, God knew the certainty of Abraham's faith and sent an angel of God from heaven to stop the act. When Abraham looked around, he saw a ram in the bush and offered it to God instead of Isaac. God blessed Abraham and promised

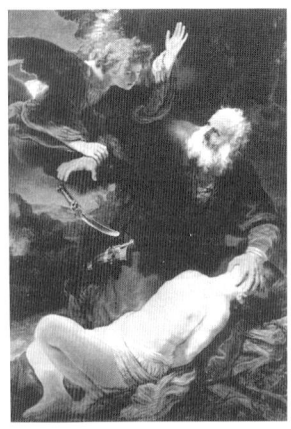

prosperity for his descendants. His wife, Sarah, died at the age of 127 shortly after the incident, perhaps because she mistakenly believed that her son had been sacrificed. Later, Abraham took a woman named Keturah as his second wife, and they had six children. Abraham, at the request of his deceased wife Sarah, gave some property to all his children except Isaac during his lifetime, and let them go to go to the eastern lands. Then

Abraham and Issac

he gave Isaac the rest of the inheritance. Isaac, at

Abraham's instruction, had taken a woman from the clan named Rebekah as his wife. Abraham lived a long life and died at the age of 175. The descendants of Jacob, the son of Isaac, later flourished, becoming the 12 tribes of Israel (Jews, Hebrews). The descendants of Ishmael, the son of Hagar, and other Isaac's half-brothers later became Arabs.

### Moses Parts the Sea

The Israelites (the Hebrews), who had worked as slaves in Egypt, led by Moses, escaped from oppressive Egypt and headed east to Mount Sinai. But Pharaoh was angry and led 600 chariots and the entire army of Egypt to pursue the Israelites. Eventually, Pharaoh caught up with the Israelites camping near the Red Sea. The Israelites blamed Moses, saying, "What the hell have you done, wouldn't it have been better for us to stay and work as slaves in Egypt than to die here?" Moses said, "Do not be afraid, calm down and see the Lord's salvation for everyone today, for you will never see the faces of the Egyptians again."

Moses 1

Then the Lord said to Moses, "Why do you shout at me? Tell the people of Israel to depart. Lift up your stick high, point your hand toward the sea, and divide the sea into two. The Israelites could cross the dry part of the sea. But water will flow over the pursuing Pharaoh's Egyptian army, over chariots and cavalry." When the Israelites crossed the sea, Moses again stretched out his hand to the sea. Then the sea flowed back to its original form before dawn.

Moses 2

The Egyptian army fled from the flow of water, but the Lord threw them into the sea. The water returned and covered the entire army, including chariots, cavalry, and the Pharaoh. They all drowned, leaving not a single one to survive. The Hebrews proceeded through the dry part of the sea, and at that time the water became the right and left walls to protect them. Thus, the Lord saved the Israelites from the oppression of the Egyptians that day. They saw many Egyptians dead on the beach. The people feared the Lord, and believed in Him and his servant Moses.

## The Ten Commandments

Moses received the so-called Ten Commandments from Yahweh (=Jehovah, God) on Mount Sinai.

1. Thou shalt have no other gods before me.

2. Thou shalt not make unto thee any graven image, or any likeness of any thing that is in heaven above, ...Thou shalt not bow down thyself to them, nor serve them: for I the Lord thy God am a jealous God, ...

3. Thou shalt not take the name of the Lord thy God in vain,

4. Six days shalt thou labour, and do all thy work: ... But the seventh day is the sabbath of the LORD thy God: in it thou shalt not do any work, thou, nor thy son, nor thy daughter, ...

5. Honour thy father and thy mother:

6. Thou shalt not kill.

7. Thou shalt not commit adultery.

8. Thou shalt not steal.

9. Thou shalt not bear false witness against thy neighbour.

10. Thou shalt not convert thy neighbour's house, thou shalt not convert thy neighbour's wife, nor his manservant, nor his maidservant, nor his ox, …

## King David

The story of King David is found in the first and second "Samuel," and in the first "Chronicles" in the Old Testament. The Old Testament is also a history book that describes the long history of the Jewish people. David, a beautiful boy from Bethlehem who was a shepherd, served Saul, king of Israel, by playing the lyre and healing the king. One day, when David went to deliver food to the battlefield, he was provoked by Goliath, the strongest warrior of the enemy soldiers. David decided to fight one-on-one and killed and beheaded Goliath. After that, David won every battle and became popular. King Saul came to hate David and often tried to kill

King David 1

him. David married Saul's daughter Michal, but the king ordered his vassals to kill David. David's vassals advised David to kill the king, but David refused. Later, the king and his sons were defeated in battle, and most of them died in battle or killed themselves. David received an oracle from God and became king of Judah, but repeatedly fought with Saul's son Ish-bosheth, who succeeded Saul as king of Israel. But on one occasion, Ish-bosheth was killed by a vassal while taking a nap. David established his capital in Jerusalem and became king of Israel and Judah, reigning as the great king for 40 years. However, in his later years, David became corrupt and entered into an affair with the wife of a vassal, fearing that her pregnancy would be discovered, he sent her husband to the battlefield and killed him in battle. David also came to think of the kingdom as his own, not God's. David chose his son Solomon as his successor before he died. Solomon also became king of Israel and Judah. And Solomon again indulged himself with worldly pleasures and disobeyed God. After Solomon's death, his son Rehoboam inherited the throne, but only two of the twelve tribes obeyed the new king, belonging to the southern kingdom of Judah. The northern ten tribes were ruled by a different king named Jeroboam as the independent kingdom of Israel. David, Solomon, and Rehoboam did not keep God's teachings and turned to idolatry. Eventually, the kingdom of Judah was attacked and destroyed by other nations, and most of the people were taken captive to Babylon. Every historical Jewish hero is depicted as a person with sinful human weakness,

King David 2

and they are not deified. The cycle of human sin, God's wrath and punishment, disobedience against God, conquest and slavery by other peoples, and God's forgiveness and salvation is repeated many times. Each time, the Jews reflected on their sins and strengthened the Torah (Jewish law). The devil is a fallen angel, and the significance of the existence of evil is interpreted as God giving man bitter trials. At the same time, we can read the context that human free will, wisdom, and idolatry generally lead to corruption. Eventually, the Jewish kingdom was conquered by the Roman Empire.

## Book of Esther

It was during the reign of King Ahasuerus of the Persian Empire, who ruled 127 provinces from India to Ethiopia. The king ascended the throne in the fortified city of Susa. The king held a banquet in the gardens of the royal palace and entertained everyone. On the seventh day, the king, who was in a good mood with wine, ordered his vassals to summon the queen Vashti, but the queen disobeyed the king's order and refused to come to the feast. The king asked his entourage how the queen should be treated according to the country's decree if she disobeyed the king's orders, and as a result, seven ministers examined and advised that if the queen's case became known throughout the country, the women all over the country would look at their husbands with contempt. Therefore, they said, Vashti should be forbidden to appear before King Ahasuerus henceforth, and that the title of queen should be given to another excellent woman, so that all the women of the world, regardless of their status, would respect their husbands, and the king agreed. The king, whose anger had subsided, decided to look for a beautiful maiden with the advice of his vassals. So, he sent officers to all the provinces of his kingdom to gather all the beautiful maidens in Susa the citadel, and decided to choose a queen. In the fortress city of Susa lived a Jew named Mordecai. His relatives had a daughter named Esther, who had lost her parents, and he had adopted her as his own daughter. Esther was beautiful in appearance and facial features, and was called to the royal palace. Esther had been told by Mordecai not to reveal that she was of Jewish origin, so she did. Eventually, she was desired by the king and became

Esther

queen instead of Vashti. The king had a high-ranking official named Haman, who hated the Jews for not kneeling before anyone but God. Because Mordecai, the Jew, did not pay homage to him at the gates of the royal palace, Haman wanted to kill all the Jews in the country. Haman, with the permission of the king, issued a decree addressed to the governors of the provinces and the chiefs of each ethnic group, announcing that on the thirteenth day of the Jewish month of Adar (around the third month of the solar calendar), the Jews, young and old, men and women, would be murdered, exterminated, and their property would be taken away.

Mordecai explained the crisis of the Jews to Esther through a person, and told her to go to the king and plead for generous treatment. But when Esther replied that even the queen would be punished by law if she approached the king in the inner court without being summoned, Mordecai replied, "You have become queen for this occasion." So, Esther went to the king, prepared to die. Esther dressed up and went into the depths of the palace, where the king held out the golden scepter in his hand to her so that she may live. This action spared her the death penalty. The king said, "Queen Esther, I will give you half of the kingdom if you wish." Then Esther invited the king and Haman to a banquet. Haman became ecstatic when he was honored to receive the invitation for two days. On the other hand, Haman had a tall pillar erected to hang Mordecai. That night, unable to sleep, the king gave orders to bring the book of memorable deeds, the chronicles of the court, and learned that Mordecai prevented the king's assassination plot. At the banquet, Esther announced that she was Jewish and begged to spare the lives of the Jewish people. The king understood the situation and arrested Haman. The king ordered to hang Haman on a pillar that Haman had built to hang Mordecai.

Mordecai, who had gained the king's trust and became a powerful official, recalled the document of the extermination of the Jews. On the contrary, decreed that on that day, the Jews of every town could assemble together, kill and exterminate every single one of the people who persecuted the Jews, including women and children, and seize their property. In fact, in the city of Susa, 500 people, including 10 of Haman's sons, were killed on the 13th. In the provinces of the kingdom, 75,000 people were killed in total. Mordecai designated the 14th and 15th as the days of blessing and feast for the Jews. It continues to this day as "Purim," where the Jews dress up and enjoy the festival.

## Malachi

FOR, behold, the day cometh, that shall burn as an oven; and all the proud, yea, and all that do wickedly, shall be stubble: and the day that cometh shall burn them up, saith the LORD of hosts, that it shall leave them neither root nor branch. But unto you that fear my name shall the Sun of righteousness arise with healing in his wings; and ye shall go forth, and grow up as calves of the stall. And ye shall tread down the wicked; for they shall be ashes under the soles of your feet in the day that I shall do this, saith the LORD of hosts. Remember ye the law of Moses my servant, which I commanded unto him in Horeb for all Israel, with the statues and judgments. Behold, I will send you Elijah the prophet before the coming of the great and dreadful day of the

LORD: And he shall turn the heart of the fathers to the children, and the heart of the children to their fathers, lest I come and smile the earth with curse.[5]

The last chapter of the Old Testament is the Book of Malachi. Malachi (Malachias) is the author's name, which means "my messenger" in Hebrew. In other words, he was a "messenger of God." At that time, Judah was under the control of the Persian Empire and suffered from heavy

Malachi

taxation. People were beginning to wonder if God really existed. The people of Israel (the Jews) had forgotten God's love, had lost their faith, had become lazy because the law was too strict, and worship in the temple had become a burden. The offering was also a burden. In such a situation, the Book of Malachi reminds people once again of God's love, reminds them of the teachings of Moses, and encourages them to obey God. Malachi declares that God will judge the evil and the arrogant, and will surely reward those who fear and honor Him, and finally, He will send the Savior, the Prophet Elijah (Hebrew for My God). Elijah appears in The First Book of the Kings (Chapters 17 to 19) and The Second Book of the Kings (Chapters 1 to 2) of the Old Testament. It is possible to speculate that some Christians regard Jesus Christ as the advent of Elijah, who is described in the last part of the Old Testament.

## The New Testament

### The Life of Jesus Christ

Jesus Christ, the linchpin of the New Testament, was repeatedly prophesied of His appearance in the following books of the Old Testament.

Isaiah 7.14: Therefore, the Lord himself will give you a sign. Behold, the virgin shall conceive and bear a son, and shall call his name Immanuel. [6]

Jeremiah 23-5:

Behold, the days are coming, declares the LORD, when I will raise up for David a righteous Branch, and he shall reign as king and deal wisely, and shall execute justice and righteousness in the land. [7]

Micah 5-2:

But you, O Bethlehem Ephrathah,

who are too little to be among the clans of Judah,

from you shall come forth for me

one who is to be ruler in Israel,

whose coming forth is from of old,

from ancient days. [8]

Zechariah 9-9:

Rejoice greatly, O daughter of Zion!

Shout aloud, O daughter of Jerusalem!

Behold, your king is coming to you;

> righteous and having salvation is he,
>
> humble and mounted on a donkey,
>
> on a colt, the foal of a donkey.[9]

Annunciation

The life of Jesus Christ is described in the Gospel of St. Matthew, the Gospel of St. Mark, the Gospel of St. Luke (he is said to have been a physician in Syria. He was a lifelong bachelor and lived to be 84 years old), and the Gospel of St. John in the New Testament. In the Gospel of St. Matthew (he is one of the 12 apostles, a tax collector of the Roman Empire), Jesus Christ is depicted as "the son of David," "the son of Abraham," "King of the Jews," "a governor, that shall rule my people Israel," "the Son of God," "Lord," "the Christ," "the Son of God," and "the Son of man." And the name "Jesus" is the most common. Mark was only a teenage boy when Jesus was executed, and he was a missionary traveler with Paul. In the Gospels, there are prominent expressions in which Jesus Himself refers to Himself as the "Son of Man." In the Gospel of St. Mark, Jesus is expressed as "Jesus Christ," "the Son of God," and "the Son of Man," "Master," "the Christ," "the Son of the Blessed," and so on.

Mary and Baby Jesus

Jesus in the desert

... NOW when Jesus was born in Bethlehem of Judæa in the days of Herod the king, behold, there came wise men from the east to Jerusalem, 2 Saying, Where is he that is born King of the Jews? for we have seen his star in the east, and come to worship him. 3 When Herod the king had heard these things, he was troubled, and all Jerusalem with him. [10]

Jesus is said to have been born in Bethlehem (south of Jerusalem) in the kingdom of Judah, which was ruled by the Roman Empire. His father was Joseph, a carpenter and a descendant of Abraham and David and his mother was Mary, a descendant of David. Jesus was born in a barn. As soon as he was born, Jesus fled to Egypt to escape the massacre of infants by Herod the Great (Matthew 2-16), and after the king's death, he lived in a city called Nazareth. At the age of 12, he already understood the Old Testament.

Sermon on the Mount

Jesus and his disciples at the Last Supper

He met John the Baptist and was baptized in the Jordan River. He was then sent out into the wilderness by the Spirit, fasted for 40 days, and was tempted by the devil (Matthew 4-1). When Jesus was over 30 years old, He went to Galilee and began mission. He preached mainly to the lower classes and the discriminated people (the handicapped, the lepers, the unclean, the marginalized, the abandoned, and the mentally ill people) about God's salvation, unconditional love, and love for the enemy. Also he rejected legalism (because Jesus thought the law is for man, not man for the law). He

Pilatus says, "Behold the man!"

declared that "all food is pure" for what should not be eaten according to the commandments, and emphasized respect for human beings rather than institutions. And he preached the grace of God earnestly. After that, he entered Jerusalem. Jesus, hated by Jewish priests, was sued and judged by the Roman Empire. Jesus was arrested by the treachery of Judas Iscariot, one of the twelve disciples of Jesus Christ (Peter, Andrew, James=John's brother, John, Philip, Bartholomew, Matthew, Thomas, James=son of Alphaeus,

Jesus on the cross

Simon the Zealot, Judas Iscariot, and Jude=Judas of Jacob). Peter and Andrew were brothers and former fishermen, and Peter later became the leader of the early Christians. John, the son of a fisherman was the youngest of the twelve and the author of the Gospel of John. The suspicious Thomas, the former tax collector Matthew, Jesus' cousin James, the most unknown Simon, and Jesus' treasurer Judas. Jesus was crucified and killed by Roman law on the hill of Golgotha outside Jerusalem. The Roman governor stated that he saw no

Golgotha, the site of Jesus' crucifixion

justification for Jesus' guilt; yet he ordered Jesus' execution at the request of the Jews. The disciples who came to Jerusalem with Jesus fled for fear of being involved. Peter, the first disciple, also ran away on the night of Jesus' arrest, saying he did not know Jesus, three times

Jesus' Resurrection

(Peter was later martyred by being crucified upside down). On the third day after Jesus' death, the women found the tomb empty, and an angel told them that Jesus had risen from the dead. Before his death, Jesus preached for only three years. Jesus Christ, who was both the Son of God and the Son of Man, must have had the recognition that men and women of all ages, ethnicities, and people with and without disabilities, are all variations of humanity. In other words, the concept that "you and I are equal each other before Almighty God" runs through the bottom of every world.

## The Life of Paul the Apostle

If the first half of the New Testament is the Gospels of the disciples about the life of Jesus, the second half is dominated by the Epistles written by Saint Paul. The passionate Paul was one of the most important apostles in the $1^{st}$ century, who traveled tirelessly from place to place and preached to not the Jews but to the non-Jews. He wrote many letters to Christians in various places. Some scholars have suggested that some of the letters may not be Paul's ones. Nevertheless, many scholars agree that the seven letters are definitely Paul's, that is to say, "The Epistle to the Romans," "The First Epistle to the Corinthians," "The Second Epistle to the Corinthians," "The Epistle to the Galatians," "The Epistle to the Philippians," "The First Epistle to the Thessalonians," and "The Epistle to Philemon."

THOUGH I speak with the tongues of men and of angels, and have not charity, I am become as sounding brass, or a tinkling cymbal. 2 And though I have the gift of prophecy, and understand all mysteries, and all knowledge; and though I have all faith, so that I could remove mountains, and have not charity, I am nothing. 3 And though I bestow all my goods to feed the poor, and though I give my body to be burned, and have not charity, it profiteth me nothing. 4 Charity suffereth long, and is kind; charity envieth not; charity vaunteth not itself, is not puffed up, 5 Doth not behave itself unseemly, seeketh not her own, is not easily provoked, thinketh no evil; 6 Rejoiceth not in iniquity, but rejoiceth in the truth; 7 Beareth all things, believeth all things, hopeth all things, endureth all things.[11]

Also, in the Epistle to the Corinthians, Paul declares that Jesus was resurrected (raised from the dead), and that Jesus Christ will come from heaven during Pau's lifetime, and expresses an eschatology in which every Christian will change into an immortal body. That is, around 50 years, Paul wrote in the letter that there would be the second coming of Christ during his lifetime.

22 For as in Adam all die, even so in Christ shall all be made alive. 23 But every man in his own order: Christ the firstfruits;

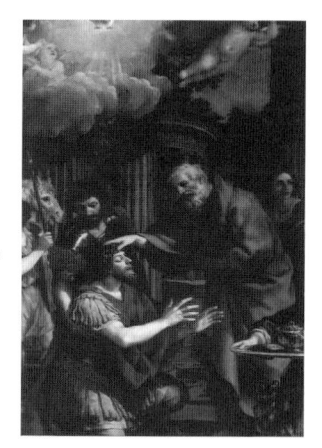

Ananias restoring the sight of St. Paul

afterward they that are Christ's at his coming. 24 Then cometh the end, when he shall have delivered up the kingdom to God, even the Father; when he shall have put down all rule and all authority and power. 25 For he must reign, till he hath put all enemies under his feet. 26 The last enemy that shall be destroyed is death.[12]

Paul (5-67 AD) was born into a wealthy Jewish family in the city of Tarsus, the capital of the province of Cilicia, Asia Minor (Turkey). Paul, who had Roman citizenship, initially persecuted Christians. Paul cracked down on a large number of Christians, and he witnessed Christians being stoned. He fully cooperated in putting Christians in prison. One day, on the way to Damascus, Jesus appeared, who was supposed to be dead, and Paul's eyes became blind, and eventually, having an "eye-opening" experience, Paul was converted and became a passionate Christian.

He traveled the Hellenistic world, from southern Turkey to Rome, including Cyprus, Philippi (an old Greek city), Athens, Corinth, Jerusalem, Crete, Malta, and Sicilia. He concluded that "Jesus is the Son of God, that He bore our original sin, and that He was crucified on behalf of people in order to save all mankind." Paul also added, "Those who believe in Jesus Christ, the Lord, will be saved." Despite being persecuted, Paul made a great contribution to spreading Christianity to non-Jewish pagans. He was placed under house arrest, under the watchful eye of Roman soldiers in his rented home in Rome. Acquitted by Emperor Nero, he was released and preached to Spain and Macedonia. He was imprisoned in Macedonia and arrested in Jerusalem. When a great fire broke out in Rome in 64, Emperor Nero began a large-scale persecution, blaming Christians for it, and Paul, who was preaching in Nicopolis, was arrested as the main culprit of the arson and taken to Rome and imprisoned. Nero's sentence was to be beheaded. Thus, Paul became a martyr.

## The General Epistle of Jude (Judas)

The insertion of Jude's short letter just before the book of Revelation is rich in metaphors. Jude is not Judas, who sold Jesus to the chief priest and elders of Judaism for only 30 pieces of silver, but Jude (Judas), the son of James, the leader of early Christianity. This Epistle warns us not to be misled by suspicious people and false prophets who claim to be Christians.

17 But beloved, remember ye the words which were spoken before of the apostles of our Lord Jesus Christ; 18 How that they told you there should be mockers in the last time, who should walk after their own ungodly lusts. 19 These be they who separate themselves, sensual, having not the Spirit. 20 But ye, beloved, building up yourselves on your most holy faith, praying in the Holy Ghost, 21 Keep yourselves in the love of God, looking for the mercy of our Lord Jesus Christ unto eternal life. 22 And of some have compassion, making a difference: 23 And others save with fear, pulling them out of the fire; hating even the garment spotted by the flesh.[13]

## The Revelation of St. John the Devine

John was the younger brother of James, a fisherman on the Sea of Galilee, and is said to be Christ's most beloved disciple. It is said that when Jesus was crucified, he was the only disciple who was under the cross. John lived a long life and died around 100 AD. In the name of John, the New Testament contained a prophetic content called "Revelation" at the end. It was an apocalypse of Jesus Christ, and something that was supposed to happen soon, something that God communicated to Christ, and that Christ communicated to John using an angel.

> Fear not, I am the first and the last, and the living one. I died, and behold I am alive forevermore, and I have the keys of Death and Hades. Write therefore the things that you have seen, those that are and those that are to take place after this.[14]

First, there were John's seven letters addressed to seven churches of Christianity in ancient Asia Minor. The locations of the seven churches were all in the cites of western Turkey: Ephesus, Izmir facing the Aegean Sea, Pergamon, Thyatira, Sardis, Philadelphia, and Laodicea (Laodikeia). John then described endlessly the visions that he saw in God's world, or visions that seemed to symbolize events that had occurred in human history. He warned that the future of human history was a future of terrible wars, including the final

war. He said that the final trial that God is about to test the people who live on earth, is coming to the whole world. And the final judgment will be handed down. Depending on the interpretation, it does not seem to be talking about the future, but rather about the history of mankind up to now in a comprehensive and symbolic way. However, in a direct sense, it can be understood as depicting an eschatological worldview, and for readers who

St. John

have been reading the Bible closely from the

beginning to the end, the sense of tension and crisis is heightened to the utmost in the final book, and it is suitable as a climax as the ending of the entire vast Bible story, including the Old Testament.

The Whore of Babylon

In the scene where the Lamb (Jesus Christ) opened the seven seals, various phenomena will occurred. When the first seal was opened, a white horse, a symbol of victory, appeared, with a crowned person straddling the horse's saddle, and holding a bow. When the second seal was opened, a red horse appeared, and the one who was given a large sword, stole the peace, killed each other, and brought war, was straddling the horse's saddle. Opening the third seal, a black horse, a symbol of famine, appeared, and the rider was holding a scale in his hand. When the fourth seal was opened, a pale horse came out, and the name of the rider was called "Death," and he was given the authority to destroy man on earth. When the fifth seal was opened, the souls of martyrs who had lost their lives for their faith appeared, and when they asked God for blood revenge, they were told to wait a while. When the sixth seal was opened, it was announced that a great earthquake and natural calamity would occur, and that the day of the great wrath of God and the Lamb would come. When the seventh seal was opened, silence was heard, and seven angels were given seven trumpets that brought calamities to the people, and another angel having a golden censer appeared. As incense was passed and the prayers of all saints were offered, thunder, lightning, and earthquakes occurred.

In preparation for a war against God, the kings of the world, who had

The Last Judgement

been deceived by evil spirits, had gathered at a place called Armageddon. And there would be lightning, thunder, and great earthquakes, and large hail would fall from heaven, and Babylon the Great would be judged. The kings of the earth, who were drunk with the wine of her obscene deeds, would be defeated by the people of Almighty God.

In the future, Satan, the devil, the old serpent, and the giant dragon will be seized and bound by God, and the kingdom will be peacefully reigned with Christ for 1,000 years, but after 1,000 years passes, Satan and his follows will be released from their prisons and they will begin to fight back. They will surround the king's city, but fire will descend from heaven and they will be all burned to the ground. And the Last Judgment will take place. The dead will be judged according to their deeds.

16 I Jesus have sent mine angel to testify unto you these things in the churches. I am the root and the offspring of David, and the bright and morning star. 17. And the Spirit and the bride say, Come. And let him that heareth say, Come. And let him that is athirst come. And whosoever will, let him take the water of life freely. 18 For I testify unto every man that heareth the words of prophecy of this book, If any man shall add unto these things, God shall add unto him the plagues that are written in this book: 19 And if any man shall take away from the words of this book of this prophecy, God shall take away his part out of the book of life, and out of the holy city, and from the things which are written in this book. 20 He which testifieth these things saith, Surely I come quickly. Amen. Even so, come, Lord Jesus. 21 The grace of our Lord Jesus Christ be with you all. Amen.[15]

Those who believe in God will be saved, Christ will come again, and the true reign of heaven, where God and people will live together, will begin. It is said that there is no death or grief there. The book of Revelation was written around 95-96 AD, nearly 30 years after St. Paul's death, and takes the form of God's new prophecy expressed through the apostle of John (He is not the same John who once baptized Jesus).

# 9. Augustine: The Great Church Father

Aurelius Augustine

After the period of Hellenism, the Roman Empire appeared. And the next big wave after ancient Greek philosophy was Christian theology. Later, the European medieval world would be an era in which Christianity dominated every state, but the theology that swept European medieval society was deeply connected to Greek philosophy and other philosophical claims, such as Epicureanism (hedonism), Stoicism, and mysticism (gnosis) from the East. Various philosophies and ideological assertions were considered to have been incorporated and systematized as theology.

Christianity was deeply engraved in European culture and history, and had a tremendous impact. Therefore, here is a brief look back at its history. Primitive Christianity, which first began as a local religion in Judea (the southern part of ancient Palestine) after the death of Jesus Christ, would later grow into a universal religion throughout Europe. And efforts to do so began with Paul (Paulos, Paul the Apostle, or Saint Paul). Christianity, which had been a mere crude Jewish religion, was fused with the essence of ancient philosophy and rationalized. Paul placed particular emphasis on the term "Holy Spirit," which was later combined with God the Father and the Son of God (Jesus Christ), leading to the "Trinity." There were many Church Fathers of the early days making great efforts. Among them, the great Church Father was Aurelius

Augustine (354-430 AD). He is the first giant of Christian theology. During his career, the Roman Empire had already recognized Christianity (313 AD) and then recognized it as the state religion (380 AD) in order to use Christian power to strengthen the weakened Roman Empire. As a result, Augustine's theological theory was strengthened. It was through him that Christianity came to a theology systematized and armed with theory that could be comparable to traditional philosophy.

Augustine was born in North Africa (present-day Algeria), a Roman colony, in 354 AD. His father was a pagan, but his mother was a devout Christian. Augustine lived at the end of the Roman Empire. That is, the Empire was divided into East and West in 397 AD, and the Western Roman Empire was destroyed in 476 AD, when the classical cultures of Greco-Rome were being destroyed by the great migration of the Germanic peoples. By the way, the Eastern Roman Empire (Byzantine Empire) survived until the 15th century, when overthrown by the Ottoman Empire (1453). Befitting these troubled times, Augustine, too, led a turbulent life. As a young man, he drowned in lust and led a life of indulgence. He believed in Manichaeism, which originated from Zoroastrianism, and became a skeptic. Later, he learned about Plato and Neo-Platonism, and the idea that there exists something transcendent beyond the human spirit led him to become a Christian and completely abandoned the hedonistic life. He knew that the true thing existed outside of his life. In 391 AD, he became a priest in the North African city of Hippo, and later became a bishop of Hippo. He strove to establish the doctrine of the Christian Church. He argued that "believing" is important in order to "know," and advocated salvation by the divine grace. He emphasized the Church and the Pope (representing Jesus).

One of Augustine's major roles in theorizing Christianity was the doctrine of the Trinity. There are three divine persons: God the Father, God the Son (Jesus Christ), and God the Holy Spirit. However, Arianism, which is now considered heretical by all modern mainstream branches of Christianity, denied the divinity of Christ and had a great influence on the Christian church at that time. Augustine criticized the Arians and advocated the Trinity. After all, Arianism was condemned as heresy at the Council of Nicaea (an ancient Greek city), and Augustine's Trinitarianism was recognized as a legitimate doctrine. Another major role of Augustine's thought was the framing of "eschatology" as a consequence of the battle between the "kingdom of God" and the "kingdom of the earth." Eschatology is central to Christian thought and is known as the Last Judgment. From an eschatological standpoint, time is a history for salvation. The kingdom of God will not be realized by the birth of Christ, but at the time of Christ's second coming, and at that time the "gospel" will spread everywhere. Of course, there are those who cannot participate in this relief. Finally, those who do not belong to the kingdom of God through the Last Judgment will face eternal death, which is called the second death. There was no idea of eschatology in Greek thought. Augustine's regard to history toward the end (eschatology), gave the history a purpose and meaning for the first time. Augustine played a major role in bringing a new sense into history, considering that his idea gives the meaning of progress to history. Still, Augustine was a person who lived in turbulent times. He took the method of finding eternal truth in doubt, and he valued revelation. In this sense, Augustine was greatly influenced by ancient Greek philosophy and the mystical Zoroastrianism. He wrote *Confessiones*, *De Civitate Dei contra Paganos* (*The Kingdom of God*), *Trinitarianism*, etc. He died at the age of 76, in 430 AD.

# 10. The Dawn of Modern History

The Renaissance began in Italy in the 14th century. Suddenly, the revival of classics blossomed as if cutting the weir of a long sleep of art and science. Until then, classics in ancient Greece and Rome had been held down for a long time by the Christian view of the world. The Renaissance means "reproduction" or "revival" in French. But the meaning strongly suggests "human revival." The main theme was to affirm humanity, that is, humanism. Renaissance humanism was a bold and powerful one, as exemplified by Leonardo da Vinci (1452-1519), who was interested in all elements of humans. Unlike subsequent humanism, Renaissance people did not focus on human weakness. Italians got out of the pressure of the Christian worldview in the Middle Ages, and they welcomed this sense as a detonator of European civilization. In 1510, Copernicus (1473-1543) publicized the heliocentric theory: the sun is the center of the solar system, and the earth is moving, not the sun. Galileo Galilei (1564-1642) was born in Pisa, Italy.

Leonardo da Vinci

Galileo excelled in mathematics, physics, and astronomy. And also, with a telescope he discovered sunspots, Jupiter's four moons, and Saturn's rings. As a scientist, Galileo argued for Copernicus' heliocentric theory, which caused the repression from the Roman Church. There is a famous anecdote that Galileo said, "The earth is still moving," after being convicted in 1633. Later, he discovered the fallen law, which led to Newton's law of universal gravitation. The

Galileo Galilei

famous "Experiment of the Leaning Tower of Pisa" is one of his experiments at that time. The 16th century in Europe was a major turning point that would completely transform the world. It was also the dawn of the Age of Great Voyages. Many Europeans, especially Portuguese and Spanish, began to explore Africa and Asia. Christopher Columbus (1451?-1506) was the first European to land in America in 1492. In fact, Columbus landed on an island off the east coast of the North American continent, called San Salvador Island.

Galileo before the Holy Office

Then England, France, and the Netherlands began to explore North America. Sir Francis Drake (1543-96) was the first Englishman to sail around the world. European countries were transitioning to modernized ones.

Leaning Tower of Pisa

In England, influenced by European literature, Geffrey Chaucer (1343?-1400) wrote *The Canterbury Tales*, whose composition is the same as *Decameron* written by Boccaccio (1313-75). Chaucer introduced many interesting English people's characters. Sir Thomas More (1478-1535) wrote *Utopia*. Then, Francis Bacon (1561-1626) published many philosophical books, saying "knowledge is power." At that time, England was ruled by Queen Elizabeth I (1533-1603) and in her reign, the playwright William Shakespeare (1564-1616) appeared like a brilliant star in the dark sky. England defeated the Spanish Armada in 1588. Elizabeth I, known as the Virgin Queen, became a symbol of modern Britain. Shakespeare became a representative of the Renaissance in England. Shakespeare has had a profound influence on the world of theater and

Christopher Columbus

literature. No great writer exceeding Shakespeare has come out afterwards. In the history of the English language, Shakespeare's English belongs to Early Modern English. However, it remains an enduring influence on the subsequent history of English for the future of the global language we are heading for.

Sir Isaac Newton (1642-1727) graduated from the University of Cambridge, and in 1665, he discovered the law of gravity, or the notion of gravitation, by watching an apple fall from a tree. He first chose Latin as the language of his study, but later he wrote his dissertations in English. At the beginning of the 16th century, Latin dominated the language of learning in Europe. It was more authoritative and much richer than any

other European languages. However, with the growth of education and the improvement of printing technology, more and more people began to read books, and they wanted to read books in their own languages. Man changed his concern from "God" to "himself." People began to have a clear view of things, that is, a scientific spirit. It is a strong human interest and scientific spirit that have characterized Europeans since the 14th century.

SHAKESPEARE

William Shakespeare

# 11. History of France, Part I

The Celts, who lived in central Europe from around the 5th century BC, came and settled in what is now France before the Greeks and Romans ruled there. The Celts (Gauls) built their own culture with leaders called druids at the top, and their life was centered on agriculture using extremely fertile land. They took advantage of the natural terrain and built forts on the hills. When the land became a province of the Roman Empire, amphitheaters, semicircular theaters, public baths, and aqueducts were built. The grain produced supported the vast amount of food for the Roman army, and the wine from Gallia (Caesar named the land "Gallia") was famous in Rome. Around this time, the mixture of Romans and Celts also progressed. In the 5th century AD, the Franks, one of the Germanic tribes living in the middle Rhine, occupied and ruled the land, which had previously been a Roman province. "Frank," which later became the origin of the present-day country's name (République française), is a Latin word meaning "brave" or "bold." They built the kingdom of the Franks (=the Frankish kingdom) and replaced the Romans as the ruling class. However, the Germanic people made up only about

Mont Saint-Michel

Château de Chambord

5 percent of the population at the time.

The Roman Empire was divided into the Eastern Roman Empire and the Western Roman Empire in 395, and the Western Roman Empire collapsed due to the oppression of Germanic tribes in 476. In the first half of the $6^{th}$ century, the Frankish kingdom controlled almost all of Gaul (Gallia), encompassing the Iberian Peninsula in the south, present-day Denmark in the north, and present-day Hungary in the east. Later, the Frankish kingdom was divided into the Middle Frankish Kingdom, the East Frankish Kingdom, and the West Frankish Kingdom. Louis I's eldest son ruled Middle Francia (Middle Frankish Kingdom), his third son, Louis II, ruled East Francia (East Frankish Kingdom), and his fourth son, Charles II, ruled West Francia (West Frankish Kingdom). Geographically, Middle Francia later became present-day Italy, East Francia became present-day Germany, and West Francia became present-day France. In the $9^{th}$ century, West Francia was terribly damaged by Viking predation, and during the reign of Charles III, the king granted land and allowed them to settle there on the condition that they stop plundering and convert to Christianity. The area became the Duchy of Normandy, and the people living there became known as the Normans. They would later become the members of the royal family and aristocrats of England.

In the 14th and 15th centuries, France fought the war against England called the "Hundred Years' War" (the war turned into a counterattack with the appearance of Joan of Arc, the daughter of a wealthy peasant of Donrémy). After the war with England, King Charles VIII was obsessed with the dream of ruling Italy to become the ruler of Christendom and sent troops to Italy (1494). Francis I then made peace with the Pope in 1516 (after the Italian War resumed in 1515). In 1519, Francis I was defeated by Charles V in the election of Holy Roman Emperor, and when Charles V (who also succeeded to the throne of Spain) became emperor of the Holy Roman Empire (a multiethnic state consisting

of present-day Germany, Austria, the Czech Republic, northern Italy, and eastern France), Francis I resumed the war in Italy in 1521, but the next Henry (Henri) II gave up the war (1559). During this period, the art of Italy's Renaissance was brought to France, and splendid castles were built along the Loire River Valley, such as the Château de Chambord. The typical French Renaissance architecture, Château de Chambord, was completed in 1547, and now it

Louis XIV

is one of the most famous castles in Europe. It was originally built as a hunting lodge for Francis I, but it was then extensively rebuilt and became the largest castle in the Loire Valley. It is said that Leonardo da Vinci was involved in the design of the castle. When the castle was nearing completion, King Francis invited his rival Charles V to the castle to show off. In the $16^{th}$ century (1572), Henry IV ascended the throne, and the Bourbon dynasty began. During the reign of Louis XIV, the Sun King, who ascended the throne in 1643, an absolute monarchy was established. The king built the Palace of Versailles. During this period, France became the most powerful country in Europe.

Palace of Versailles (Château de Versailles)

# 12. **Descartes:** Cogito, Ergo Sum (I think, therefore I am)

René Descartes

René Descartes was born in La Haye en Touraine, France, in 1596. His father was a member of the Parlement of Rennes, and his mother was too weak to die a year after giving birth to Descartes. At the age of 10, he enrolled in a Jesuit school called La Flèche, where he studied conservative scholastic philosophy, theology, etc. He loved mathematics throughout his student days, graduated with honors from the academy, and entered Université de Poitiers (University of Poitiers) to study law. In 1616, he became a bachelor of law at the age of 20. He then enlisted in the army and spent time in Germany. After his return, he traveled to Venice and Rome (1623-25), and when he returned to Paris, he interacted with many scholars and philosophers. After moving to the Netherlands at the age of 32, he began to work on philosophy and write in earnest. He moved to the Netherlands because he was able to live a solitary and hidden life. Galileo Galilei (1564-1642) was once condemned by the Pope for heresy for his heliocentric theory and convicted in two trials (1616 and 1633). In order to avoid such ideological repression, Descartes may have decided to leave Catholic France and live in the Protestant Netherlands. At the age of 45 (1641), he published *Meditationes de prima philosophia* (*Meditations on First Philosophy*) in Paris. The publication of this book increased Descartes' fame, but at the same time he was denounced by theologians as being dangerous. Descartes was criticized as a "thinker who spread atheism."

In October 1649, he was invited by Queen Kristina of Sweden (1626-1689) to live in the capital city, Stockholm. He lectured for the queen but contracted a cold and got pneumonia. He died there in February 1650, at the age of 53. He published eight books during his lifetime (including after his death).

Descartes' philosophy is also a kind of Platonism. Descartes was a rational philosopher who believed in what he thought in his head rather than what he saw with his eyes.

Descartes established the basic principle of philosophy. If we compare it to mathematics, it is like discovering "1 + 1 = 2" for the first time in the world. For this achievement, Descartes is considered the father of modern philosophy. He used "methodological skepticism," a method of thoroughly doubting everything in the world, and after much doubt, he sought a universal and absolute truth that could be asserted that this doubt alone was indisputable. Everything we see might be a hallucination. All the sounds we hear could be auditory hallucinations. Right now, we cannot tell if we are awake and living in reality or if we are asleep and dreaming. We do not even know if this world really exists in the first place. It's a strange idea, but demons may be showing us a false world... Then, while doubting everything, Descartes realized that only his consciousness of doubting things definitely exists. Even if he suspected that his consciousness did not actually exist, he would not deny the fact that he himself doubted it. This is "Cogito, Ergo Sum (Je pense, donc je suis / I think, therefore I am)." This idea led to the development of modern philosophy by elucidating the structure of the world on the premise that one's own consciousness exists.

Now, Descartes made it clear that our consciousness definitely exists.

But at this point, it is not clear whether the world really exists and what the essence of things in the world is. The next task, then, is to establish an "epistemology" that examines whether we really perceive the world correctly. Investigation of the extent to which humans can correctly perceive things has become a major issue. So, Descartes coined the idea of "rationalism." "Rationalism" is the position that correct knowledge can be acquired only after thinking logically in the head. It is a Cartesian way of thinking that even if he doubted everything in the world, he could place absolute trust in his own consciousness alone. He argued that even if Man does not experience anything, he is born with a concept (innate idea), and that the conclusion drawn on the basis of it is correct knowledge. And Man is born with the concept of infinity. Then there are infinite entities. For Descartes, infinite substance is God, that is, God exists. For example, the value of pi continues indefinitely. Man cannot know all the numbers. Even if he uses a computer to calculate hundreds of millions or trillions of digits, he will not reach infinity, so

he cannot say that he has fully calculated the value of pi. But God, who is omniscient and omnipotent, naturally knows all the values of pi. What does it mean to know

Queen Kristina (left) and Descartes (right)

about the infinite numbers? It cannot be imagined by human beings, who are finite entities. But Descartes was convinced that as long as Man knew the concept of infinity, there existed an entity that knew infinity. He concluded that if God exists, Almighty God would not cause Man to have a false perception, and that Man can correctly perceive the world.

The house where Descartes was born

# 13. History of England

The British Isles were connected to continental Europe more than 10,000 years ago, but gradually, the current topography was formed after a long time. From about 5,000 BC, the Iberians, who originated in North Africa and settled in southern Europe, migrated to England and practiced cattle raising and farming. Later, from Europe, the Beakers invaded, leaving stone circles such as Stonehenge in Salisbury. The Beakers also pastured, but armed themselves with bows and arrows to prepare for foreign enemies. Later, the Celts came from the center of continental Europe, used iron (and bronze) tools and weapons instead of conventional stone and bronze ones, and built many hillforts, the earliest forms of castles at that time, on hills (around 700-500 BC). In 55-54 BC, Consul Julius Caesar, a Roman, led a fleet to invade Britain, and in 43 AD the Roman troops advanced in earnest and finally conquered all of England. The Roman army built many Roman forts, full-scale stone military installations in every place, and many Romanized cities appeared. The word "chester" is derived from the Latin words castrum (singular) and castra (plural), and refers to a military camp, but the plural form means "large encampment" and later also came to mean military fortifications. It also meant Roman Fort. The smaller fortress was called "castellum," which later became "castle." Even today, place names with "chester" at the end of the place name in various parts of England. For example, Chester, Colchester, Doncaster, Lancaster, Leicester, Manchester, Winchester, and so on.

Many Roman roads were built, and Hadrian's Wall was built on the

The Tower of London

border with Scotland in 128 AD. Pursued by the Germanic tribes invading from northwestern Europe, the Romans withdrew completely from England in 410 AD. Britain, which had been governed by the Romans, was now oppressed by the Jutes, Angles, and Saxons, who by the 6th century had driven the indigenous Celts to Wales, Scotland, and other backwaters and settled in England. They built fortified settlements called Burgs (Saxon Forts) in various places. However, unlike the Romans, they did not have stone technology, so the walled cities they built were made of wood and earth. It is a remnant of this that place names with the word "burgh" at the end of the word remain in various parts of England and Scotland even today. Examples include Edinburgh, Middlesbrough, Peterborough, and Scarborough.

Areas dominated by the Angles were called "Angle-land," which eventually became known as "England." In the 8th century, Viking invasions began from the Scandinavian Peninsula, and in 1016, King Canute of Denmark became King of England. After that, the English king became Anglo-Saxon again, but in 1066, when King Edward the Confessor died, England was immediately conquered by William, Duke of Normandy, France, and William became King William I of England. Thereafter, in England, the ruling class was Norman French and the common people were Germanic. French was spoken in castles and Anglo-Saxon in castle towns and in the countryside. Anglo-Saxon culture eventually merged with French culture, and so did the language, becoming English. English spoken in the Middle Ages was a fusion of German and French with a sentence structure based on Germany and a large influx of French vocabulary.

Norman kings constructed sturdy castles in various locations and establised a network of castles to rule over all of England. During the reign of King John (reigned 1199-1216), the French territories inherited from the previous kings were lost, and the royal power was restricted in domestic affairs, triggering the beginning of parliamentary politics.

As for Wales, it has a harsh climate and many steep mountains. The Welsh once lived in different tribes in each region, and there was no unified dynasty. Few lived in towns and villages, kept livestock, and built shabby huts woven from twigs. Battles between the tribes were constantly repeated, and when the enemy attacked, the clans packed up and fled to the forests to fight back with guerrilla warfare. There was no armor, and weapons were large bows, swords, throwing spears, etc., and it is said that they fought barefoot even in the harsh winter. Originally, most of the Welsh were the indigenous Celts of England, who once lived in the plains and fertile regions of England, but were driven to Wales by the invasions of the Romans, Anglo-Saxons, and Vikings. During the Seven Anglo-Saxon Kingdoms (Northumbria, Mercia, East Anglia, Essex, Sussex, Wessex, and Kent), Offa, King of Mercia (756-96) built a great earthen barrier on the border between England and Wales, called

Boudica, Celtic War Queen

the "Offa's Dyke," to cut off relations with the Welsh. William the Conqueror, after the conquest of England, also placed the Earl of Chester and the Earl of Shrewsbury on the border to monitor Wales. However, the border lords later invaded Wales and seized territory without the king's permission to expand their holdings. This is why early Norman noble castles and towns were established in the south and central Wales. During the reign of King Edward I (r. 1272-1307), the king completely conquered Wales and made an expedition to Scotland. During this period, fortified cities were formed in various places, and castles, cathedrals, city gates, and city walls were constructed. Edward III (r. 1327-77) sought the former French territories, which led to the Hundred Years' War between England and France (1337-1453). Then, due to the failure of the Anglo-French War, the succession to the throne problem occurred in England, and the House of Lancaster (Red Rose) and the House of York (White Rose) fought each other, resulting in the so-called Wars of the Roses (1455-85). Eventually, Henry VII of the Red Rose (r. 1485-1509) won, and the Tudor dynasty began. The next king, Henry VIII (r. 1509-47), carried out setting up his own Church of England (breaking away from the Catholic Church) due to his personal divorce problems and succeeded in modernizing England. The king built many military fortifications along the coastline in preparation for the attack from France and Spain.

Windsor Castle

After Queen Mary I, the Catholic England became Protestant again

Queen Elizabeth I

when her sister Elizabeth was the queen (r. 1558-1603), and the nation prospered even more than in the time of her father, Henry VIII, and the navy was strengthened. In 1588, English ships (sea dogs) defeated the Spanish Armada, which was praised as the strongest in Europe at the time, in the English Channel (Battle of Armada).

As overseas expansion was promoted, the East India Company (a semi-public and semi-private company) advanced to Japan via India, China, and Indonesia and opened a trading house in Hirado, Japan. Textiles and *cha* (green tea) were imported to England, and *cha* became British tea. It was also during this period that William Shakespeare (1564-1616), the world's greatest writer, was active. After Queen Elizabeth's death, James VI of Scotland became King James I of England, and his son Charles I came into conflict with Parliament, eventually leading to civil war, and the king was beheaded (1649). England became a temporary republic, but the monarchy was restored and Charles II ascended the throne (1660).

In the 18th century, a German prince, George of Hanover, the great-grandson of James I, became George I, and the Hanoverian dynasty started. All four kings went under the name of George. During this period, the Industrial

Queen Victoria

Queen Elizabeth II

Revolution occurred, and the economy developed greatly. In the 19th century, England became the world's most powerful country, and Queen Victoria, who also served as Empress of India, became a symbol of the British Empire.

During the French Revolutionary Wars (1792-1802), the victory of the British fleet, led by Horatio Nelson (1758-1805), over the French fleet at the Battle of the Nile in 1798, resulted in Napoleon being isolated in Egypt and France ceding control of the Mediterranean

Palace of Westminster

to Britain. During the Napoleonic Wars (1803-15), Nelson defeated the combined Franco-Spanish fleet at the Battle of Trafalgar in 1805 to prevent the French invasion of the British mainland. Nelson is known for sending a message saying

Buckingham Palace

"England expects that every man will do his duty." Nelson was fatally wounded and died during the battle. The message must have meant that "Nelson will do his duty." In 1815, the Duke of Wellington (Arthur Wellesley, 1st Duke of Wellington, 1769-1852) defeated Napoleon's French army at Waterloo in Belgium, and Napoleon fled to Paris, where he finally surrendered (Battle of Waterloo, Bataille de Waterloo).

England opened many colonies around the world and became the center of the British Empire. But in the 20th century, after two world wars, British colonies became independent. In the 21st century, the United Kingdom, which has become the leader of the British Commonwealth in name only, still does not lose its presence as the center of the world's leading developed countries. Then, it advocates a new lifestyle such as how to live a 100-year-old life. The British are constantly disseminating information and new ideas to the world.

Kensington Palace

## Winston Churchill

Sir Winston Churchill was Britain's most popular politician. He was a grandson of the 7th Duke of Marlborough. His father was a Conservative politician, and his mother was American. Ever since he was a child, he hated studying and his grades were the lowest in all subjects. After graduating from the Royal Military Academy Sandhurst, he published *The Story of the Malakand Field Force* based on his war experiences. In 1899, he left the army to make a living by writing and went to war as a private journalist. At the age of 26, he ran for the Conservative Party and was elected for the first time and entered politics. When World War I began, he became the head of the British Royal Navy. In 1917, he was appointed as the Minister of Munitions and worked on the development of tanks to break through the trenches. After World War I, Churchill devoted himself to anti-communist diplomacy. Churchill was so radical that he was transferred to the post of Secretary of State for the Colonies. In the general election of 1922, he was considered a belligerent politician and lost his Dundee seat. Around this time, he wrote *The World Crisis*.

Winston Churchill

He lost again in the next election. In 1924, he became Chancellor of the Exchequer and was a leading candidate for the next prime minister. When Mussolini of Italy rose to power, Churchill commented that "Fascism is the most effective antidote to the poison of the Russian Revolution." In 1929, the Wall Street Crash doubled the number of unemployed people in the UK. His autobiography, *My Early Life*, was published in 1930. On September 1, 1939, German forces invaded Poland, and Britain and France declared war on Nazi Germany. World War II began, and Churchill was appointed First Lord of the Admiralty. Eventually, public opinion became dominated by the long-awaited view that Churchill should become prime minister. In 1940, the first Churchill cabinet began. Churchill arrested fascists and communists in the country one after another. After the withdrawal of Dunkirk and the fierce battle of the British mainland called the Battle of Britain, the Normandy landings were successful on June 6, 1944. After the fall of Rome, Mussolini was captured and executed, and then Italy surrendered. After Hitler's suicide, Germany surrendered on May 8, 1945. Churchill became a national hero. In 1951, he became prime minister again (at the age of 77) and appealed to the world the presence of Britain as the important country possessing the atomic bomb after the US and the Soviet Union. From 1948, he wrote *Memoirs of the Second World War*, and in 1953, he was awarded the Nobel Prize in Literature. Churchill was the strong leader of Britain during World War II. After the rise of Hitler, while the countries of Europe bowed down to Nazism, Churchill insisted on fighting thoroughly. Britain struggled alone, fighting an all-out war, and finally won with American reinforcements. Looking back at his accomplishments, Churchill only won and lost. He used to fail and succeed. He was entrusted with many ministerial positions, but sometimes, even if he did well, his policy didn't work out. In a sense, he was just a leader. However, he was appointed as minister again and again, and eventually elected as the top wartime leader. He was thoroughly anti-communist, anti-German, and pro-American. He hated Gandhi for leading a nonviolent movement in India. Many British politicians of the time were sympathetic to Nazi Germany and were generous to Germany's demand for rearmament. The pro-Germans tried to use Germany as an anti-Soviet bulwark. Churchill, the eccentric, clearly maintained his anti-Nazi position instinctively and intuitively. And he became the best leader of Britain.

## English Literature

The UK is home to many writers. To begin with, literature is a national specialty in Britain, where Shakespeare was born. The number of literature lovers in Britain is higher than in other countries. In a country, where individualism has developed, there are many personal opinions and ideas. Sometimes, a new story is born, and sometimes it turns into a big story. The profession of writer appeared for the first time in England during the 18th and 19th centuries. In the UK, a country of class society, children took over their parents' occupation, so there are basically few opportunities to work in another profession that was different from that of their parents. However, at that time, the profession of writer, which was born as a new industry, was not hereditary. It was a growing industry, and there were many vacancies. With such a social background, the writer industry may have gained popularity at the time as a job. In any case, the true reason during Victorian era, so many writers emerged was that they needed to reach out to the non-religious who didn't go to church. The middle class became very powerful, and writers educated businesslike people who didn't want to listen to preachers' sermons any more. Novelists entertained people, and at the same time, they played the role of making people think deeply about life.

Jane Austen (1775-1817), the author of *Pride and Prejudice*, was the first female novelist in England. Mary Shelley (1797-1851) was famous for the Gothic novel *Frankenstein*. Then, the greatest Victorian novelist, Charles Dickens (1812-70), appeared, and he wrote *Oliver Twist*, *A Christmas Carol*, *David Copperfield*, *Great Expectations*, and so on. After Dickens' novels, other important Victorian literary works are *Jane Eyre* (1847) by Charlotte Brontë, *Wuthering Heights* (1847) by Emily Brontë, *Silas Marner* (1861) by George Eliot, *Alice's Adventures in Wonderland* (1865) by Lewis Carroll, *A Dog of Flanders* (1872) by Ouida, *Strange Case of Dr Jekyll and Mr Hyde* (1886) by Robert Louis Stevenson, *Tess of the D'Urbervilles* (1891) by Thomas Hardy, *The Picture of Dorian Gray* (1891) by Oscar Wilde, and *The Adventures of Sherlock Holmes* (1892) by Sir Arthur Conan Doyle. In the 20th century, D.H. Lawrence (1885-1930), the first writer from the working class, appeared, and James Joyce (1882-1941), an important writer from Dublin, the capital of Ireland, appeared. Other notable writers include Agatha Christie (1890-1976), famous for *Murder on the Orient Express* and *And Then There Were None*; Dodie Smith (1896-1990), famous for *The Hundred and One Dalmatians* (*One Hundred and One Dalmatians*); Anne Fine (1947-), famous for *Madame Doubtfire*; and the most successful female writer, J.K. Rowling (1965-), who became an astonishing best-selling author by writing the *Harry Potter* series.

Shakespeare

## The Beatles

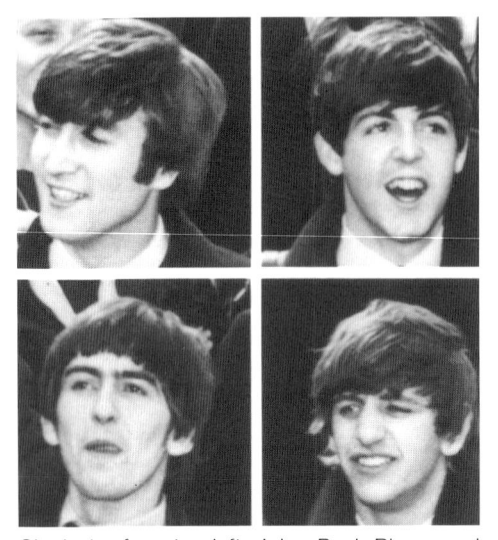

Clockwise from top left: John, Paul, Ringo, and George

If you look at the history of Western music, first, in the Middle Ages (15th-16th century), "church music" comes to mind. People sang Christian chants in churches. In the Renaissance period, "court music" became popular, in addition to religious songs. At the end of the 16th century, opera (originally based on the theatrical revival of ancient Greece) was born in Firenze, Italy. In the 17th century, Baroque music was born in Italy, and Antonio Vivaldi (1678-1741) appeared. Later, in Germany, Bach (1685-1750), whose father was a court musician, became a representative composer. Then, music spread to the general public, and "classical music" with an emphasis on form and harmony arose. Symphonies and concertos were actively performed. Haydn (1732-1809), born in Austria; Mozart (1756-91), born in Salzburg; and Beethoven (1770-1827), born in the Holy Roman Empire (Germany), were representative composers. They were followed by Romantic music with an emphasis on expression, which produced Schubert (1797-1828) in Austria, Chopin (1810-49) in Poland, Wagner (1813-83) in Leipzig in the Kingdom of Saxony (now Germany), and Dvořák (1841-1904) in the Czech Republic.

There was a composer Tchaikovsky (1840-93), who was active in Russia during the same period. It is said that the 18th-19th century was the peak of modern Western music, and its role as the only absolute standard music of the world, ended in the 1950s. In the 20th century, impressionist music expressed in terms of mood and atmosphere was born in France. Debussy (1862-1918) was a prime example. After World War II (1945-), free music called "contemporary music" occurred. In contrast to the profound and lofty Western classical music, black music, jazz was born in New Orleans, USA around 1900. Louis Armstrong (1901-71) and Duke Ellington (1899-1974) are probably the most famous. In the 1950s, jazz (blues and gospel) gave birth to rock music. The prototype of rock music was rock 'n' roll, and it is said that rock was born from the fusion of black blues and white country music. Around this time, R&B emerged from the jazz world, emphasizing the entertainment value of singing and dancing. In the 1950s, rock 'n' roll was often perceived as white music and R&B (performed by Ray Charles, for example) as black music. Mississippi rock singer Elvis Presley (1935-77) appeared in the 1950s and helped to make

The Beatles awarded the MBE (1965)

rock 'n' roll a major music that was popular with young American girls. Later, folk music emerged, influenced by the traditional country music. Bob Dylan (1941-) sang and played the guitar and harmonica, establishing a way of singing that valued poetry. In the midst of this trend, the Beatles appeared as a rock band born in Liverpool, England, in the 1960s. They brought the center of rock, or rather, the center of world-influencing music, back from the US to Europe. Specifically, it was Britain, rather than Europe, that became the new focal point of music for the first time in modern history. Indeed, in its long histroy, Britain attracted worldwide attention to its music through the sound of the Beatles. The Beatles was a rock band made up of four young guys from working-class backgrounds in Liverpool. They were John Lennon, Paul McCartney, Ringo Starr, and George Harrison. They wrote lyrics, composed, played, and sang their own songs. Not only are the songs they created masterpieces, but their individuality and their sense of humor have captivated people all over the world. There were Vivaldi in Italy, Beethoven in Germany, Tchaikovsky in Russia, and Debussy in France; England's notable contributions to popular music came much later.

After the Beatles, the center of global popular music eventually shifted back to the United States, leading to the rise of artists like Michael Jackson and others.

London Beatles Store

# 14. Francis Bacon: Knowledge is Power

Francis Bacon

Francis Bacon is the founder of British empiricism. He was born in London in 1561, a son of Sir Nicholas Bacon, Lord Keeper of the Great Seal. He attended Trinity College, Cambridge, but dropped out after two years without graduating. Bacon did not appreciate Aristotle's philosophy, as superior to discussion and controversy but not useful to human life, and increased his interest in the natural sciences. He later studied law and qualified as a barrister. At the age of 23, he became a Member of Parliament, and eventually became Chief Justice of the Supreme Court (Lord Chancellor). However, he became involved in a political trouble. He was accused of taking bribes, and he was resigned and imprisoned.

Bacon advocated "induction" as a scientific research method. In other words, it is a method of deriving general laws and universal facts from individual cases and concrete facts. He emphasized sensory experiences such as experimentation and observation. In empiricism, experience is not a personal experience but has a strong connotation of objective and public experimentation and observation. His particular emphasis on sensory and perceptual experience led to the genealogy of John Locke, George Berkley, and David Hume. Bacon's philosophy is also called "sensualism" or "sensationalism," and his empiricism later influenced "materialism" or "positivism." On the other hand, empiricism conflicts with metaphysics such as continental rationalism, intuitionism, and mysticism.

Bacon's science differs from Aristotelian scientific thought. In other words, Aristotelian science shows that Man observes nature, accumulates, organizes, and systematizes its records. However, Bacon's science argues that Man does not merely imitate nature but intervenes, manipulates, and experiments with nature. Knowledge can be obtained through experience and experiment.

They (Studies) perfect nature (human character), and are perfected by experience: for natural abilities (innate abilities) are like natural plants, that need proyning (pruning), by study; and studies themselves, do give forth directions too much at large, except they be bounded in by experience. Crafty men contemn studies, simple men admire them, and wise men use them; for they (studies) teach not their own use; but that is a wisdom without them, and above them, won by observation. ( ※ notes in parentheses are by Nishino)[16]

*Complete Essays of Francis Bacon*

Robert Dudley, Bacon's political enemy

Bacon advocated that "knowledge is power," but at the same time, he said that human beings sometimes make false perceptions due to preconceived notions and prejudices. Bacon called these notions that hinder correct perception, "Idols." And Bacon classified them into four categories. One is the Idol of the Tribe, which is a false assumption by the senses that every human being has, such as an optical illusion. Next is the

Idol of the Cave, which is a prejudice arising from the mind of an individual (personality) or from the environment in which we grow up. Next is the Idol of the Marketplace, which is a prejudice due to false gossip from people. Finally, the last one is the Idol of the Theater, which is the prejudice that arises from believing without thinking about what experts and great people say. Bacon requested people to remove these four Idols and concluded that the conclusions drawn by the induction, that is, the method of collecting cases and evidence through observation and experimentation and finding the common concepts to them, are correct knowledge.

Bacon also said, "Reading enriches people, speaking makes people agile, and writing makes people sure." Knowledge and scholarship gained through experience and experimentation make people happy. Bacon separated learning from religion, reason from faith, and he can be said to have established the basic ideas of modern natural science. He published *Essays* (1st edition 1597, 2nd edition 1612, and 3rd edition 1625), *The Advancement of Learning* (1605), *New Atlantis* (posthumously published), *Novum Organum* (*New Organon*, 1620), etc. Bacon was well versed in Latin, and many of his works were written in Latin; however, *Essays*, *The Advancement of Learning*, and *New Atlantis* were written in English, so they were widely read around the world in later generations. In his later years, he conducted an experiment with freezing by stuffing a chicken full of snow, which led him to catch a cold, from which he died in 1626 at the age of 65.

# 15. John Locke: At Birth, the Mind is a Blank Slate

John Locke

John Locke (1632-1704) was born in Somerset, southwest England, as the eldest son of John Locke, an attorney and a clerk of a magistrate in Somerset. He grew up in a Presbyterian Puritan family and attended Oxford University. He studied philosophy and medicine, earned bachelor's and master's degrees, and became a Christchurch Fellow. He tutored aristocrats and traveled to France. Then, he became a lecturer at the University of Oxford, where he taught Greek, rhetoric, and philosophy.

When Earl of Shaftesbury (1621-83), for whom Locke served as a private secretary, fled to the Netherlands, where Locke also went. Later, when the Glorious Revolution broke out in 1688, he returned to England, following Queen Mary II back (1689). Then he became an adviser to the new government, attended various meetings and committees, and cooperated with William III and his wife Queen Mary II. In the year Locke returned to England, his masterpieces were published in rapid succession, such as *An Essay Concerning Human Understanding*, *Two Treatises of Government*, and *A Letter Concerning Toleration*.

Locke advocated the idea of democracy, which eliminated the state's interference with the individual and had a great influence on liberal individualism. He insisted on the "right to revolution" and had a major influence on the later French Revolution and the American Revolution. Locke denied the nativism and took a stand against Platonism, which holds the idea that only Idea that humans are born with exist. Locke's philosophy belongs to the genealogy of nominalism (the belief that universality does not exist) that the universal exists only as the name of the thing.

> Let us then suppose the mind to be, as we say, white paper, void of all characters, without any ideas: —How comes it to be furnished? Whence comes it by that vast store which the busy and boundless fancy of man has painted on it with an almost endless variety? Whence has it all the MATERIALS of reason and knowledge? To this I answer, in one word, from EXPERIENCE. In that all our knowledge is founded; and from that it ultimately derives itself. Our observation employed either, about external sensible objects, or about the internal operations of our minds perceived and reflected on by ourselves, is that which supplies our understandings with all the MATERIALS of thinking. These two are the fountains of knowledge, from where all the ideas we have, or can naturally have, do spring.[17]

> *An Essay Concerning Human Understanding*

Locke held that the existence of God is true without any argument, but Man has no idea (knowledge) when he is born. Nothing is universal beyond experience. Man was originally born in a state of "white paper" (*tabula rasa* or blank slate), and by "experience" of perception

Queen Mary II

(accumulating various ideas), letters are written on the blank slate, and knowledge is formed. He held that there is not a single principle that all mankind can universally agree on. English empiricism was a philosophy that disliked to boast out the truth. Locke did not claim that there is no universal truth, but his idea is that different experiences have different ideas.

He published *Two Treatises of Government* (1689), *An Essay Concerning Human Understanding* (1689), *Second Treatise of Government* (1690), *Some Consideration of the Consequences of the Lowing of Interest, and Raising the Value of Money* (1692), *Some Thoughts Concerning Education* (1693), *The Reasonableness of Christianity, as Delivered in the Scriptures* (1695), etc.

After returning to England, Locke lived in London for a while, but when his health deteriorated, he moved to live in Essex, at the country house of Lady Masham (Otes House). She was Locke's close friend for a long time. Locke never married and had no children. He died at Otes House on 28 October 1704, at the age of 72.

# 16. **Wordsworth:** Let nature be your teacher

William Wordsworth

The advent of the Romantic poet William Wordsworth (1770-1850) dramatically changed the British sense of beauty towards nature. It is different from the rationalists of the continent who think nature is imperfect, or the Americans who think nature is something that man can conquer. Wordsworth's sense of nature is somewhat similar to that of Japanese people. Looking at the social background of Britain in those days, we easily noticed that people's lifestyle changed a lot since the Industrial Revolution. Science and technology moved the world drastically. Arkwright invented the water frame spinning machine, James Watt built the first efficient steam engine, and the first typewriter, telephone, electric light bulb, sewing machine, and camera were invented in Britain. Military weapons progressed, and overseas explorations were further expanded. People in Britain abandoned the countryside and came to the cities to work as laborers. Their way of thinking became utilitarian, and they began to think based on the concept of a simple profit and loss account.

Wordsworth was born in 1770 in Cockermouth (the Lake District), as the second of five children of John Wordsworth, who was a legal representative of James Lowther, $1^{st}$ Earl of Lonsdale. His mother, Anne, died of a malignant cold at the age of 30, when William was 7 years old. Five years after his

Sunset over Tintern Abbey

mother's death, his father, John, died of overwork at the age of 42. Not welcomed by relatives, William and his siblings were forced to leave their home and lost the foundation of the family. William went to St John's College, Cambridge University, but he felt alienated by being discriminated against based on status as a minority special scholarship student in a dormitory with many aristocrats and upper-class youths. While in college, he embarked on a three-month walking trip to the Alps of continental Europe. At this time, he visited France, Switzerland, and Italy. After graduating from Cambridge, he hoped to pursue a career in literature. He traveled to Wales and climbed Mount Snowdon. In 1791, he went to the continent again. This time, he wanted to learn French and become a private tutor who would take the children of the upper aristocracy on trips to France. Eventually, he met a French woman, Annette Vallon, who was four years older than him, who taught him French for free, and they became romantically involved. Vallon eventually gave birth to their daughter Caroline upon William's return to England. After that, the Anglo-French War made it impossible for him to go to France, and his dream of teaching on continental travel disappeared.

Before long, Wordsworth sympathized with William Godwin's *Political Justice* and became an atheist, supporting the French Revolution. In 1795, he published a weekly magazine, *The Philanthropist,* dealing with political criticism and political thought. However, 6 months after the publication of the magazine, Wordsworth quit publishing the magazine, and at the same time, gave up on Godwin, disliked revolutionary terrorism, and distanced himself from left-wing communism. He sought the beauty of nature and the value of everyday life. He deepened his philosophical contemplation and devoted himself to the inner soul of man, the essence of nature, and religious thoughts. He longed for a life like a recluse who lives a simple life and thinks deeply about Almighty God. In 1798, he co-authored with Samuel Taylor Coleridge (1772-1834) in *Lyrical Ballads*. Wordsworth's 'Lines written a few miles above Tintern Abbey' adorned the end of the collection of poems. The origins of Wordsworth's idea of this work, *Lyrical Ballads*, were deeply rooted in the poor and oppressed lives of the lower classes in rural areas. Every subject of poetical works was the suffering and poverty of the people. Main characters were old men, unhappy women, and unfortunate boys. There was no social relief for the poor and weak. However, Wordsworth sought salvation and healing from nature, getting close to nature, looking at himself, and deepening his thoughts. He realized that nature never betrayed him.

A visit to Tintern Abbey by moonlight

Here, I would like to give

Southern end of Derwent Water

a supplementary explanation of 'Tintern Abbey,' the best work among *Lyrical Ballads*. Although there is no actual ruined temple in the poem, the name of the temple Tintern Abbey is important and symbolic for the poet. The area of Tintern (Welsh: Tyndyrn) is on the west bank of the River Wye in Monmouthshire, Wales, just on the border between England and Wales. Of course, Wales had a sad history, that is, it was invaded and conquered by England. The Welsh are Celts, not Anglo-Saxons. The Celts, who originally lived in England, were driven out by the Anglo-Saxons and fled to the mountainous Walsh region. The temple was originally built by King Henry I of England in the 12th century, and the abbey was built in the 14th century as it remains today. However, it was abolished in the 16th century by Henry VIII's Dissolution of the Monasteries and has since fallen into disrepair. Today, however, the ruined Abbey exudes a picturesque beauty that always attracts visitors, with a sense of "tranquil restoration."

Every time visiting the ruined castles and temples that remain throughout England, we sometimes think of the gorgeous and robust buildings that were once a symbol of authority and power, but eventually crumbled with time and still exist, withstanding the wind and snow of time. But when we look at the fresh green ivy that grows vigorously on the walls of the ruined buildings, and the rich greenery of the surroundings, we still feel awe of the power of nature.

In the autumn of 1798, Wordsworth travelled to Germany with his sister Dorothy and Coleridge. In the autumn of 1799, Wordsworth and Dorothy decided to return to the Lake District, where they had spent their childhood. First, they lived in Town End, near Lake Grasmere. The house they lived in was later called "Dove Cottage." The following year, Coleridge and Robert Southey also moved to the Lake District, and the three became known as the "Lake Poets." During this period (1799-1808), Wordsworth practiced his activities as a vigorous poet. His motto was "plain living, but high thinking." According to Wordsworth's thought, if you experience walking in the great nature that has a majestic and sublime beauty, you would think that both rich and poor are the same, and there is not much difference between them as very petty human beings in the great outdoors. In the 1801 revised edition of *Lyrical Ballads*, Wordsworth declared that the language of the work would be the ordinary language used by rural people in the English countryside.

Wordsworth also warned that human beings, who were once supposed to be deeply connected to nature, were living in a way that was against nature. Originally, man was a part of nature, but

Grasmere

people have forgotten the fact. In the past, humans were taught the way to live by nature. Nature surely brings salvation to man. Humans should be closer to nature and feel the joy of living. And Wordsworth naturally felt the love of God in nature. Just as Sir Walter Scott (1771-1832) focused on the spirit of chivalry (and Christianity) in medieval history, Wordsworth sought to revive the spirit of Christianity in nature and in the countryside. Both of them were trying to show a way of life to those who had lost their humanity in a chaotic big city. A quiet and peaceful park in a metropolitan area is now an oasis for people, a place for the rebirth of our souls.

In 1802, Wordsworth married his childhood friend, Mary Hutchinson. They were blessed with five children (three of them died before Wordsworth and Mary). In 1813 they moved to "Rydal Mount," a house located in a small village of Rydal in the Lake District. Wordsworth died in the house in 1850 at the age of 80 (Mary died in 1859).

Wordsworth loved the nature of the Lake District and even published his own travelers' guidebook, *Guide to the Lake District*, but today, many tourists

  may be more familiar with Beatrix Potter's (1866-1943) *Peter Rabbit* when they think of the Lake District. *The Tale of Peter Rabbit* is a picture book for children written by Beatrix Potter. But the accuracy and quality of its

Beatrix Potter       Peter Rabbit (left)       illustrations must have

captured the hearts of not only children but also many adults. Beatrix was very good at drawing. Originally, she loved drawing from an early age, kept various animals as pets, was interested in mushrooms as a young biologist, and had the skill of accurately sketching. Her anthropomorphic rabbits and other animals are basically realistic, but at the same time added cuteness. It looks like a real rabbit with a human heart and human manners added to it. And it's as if the rabbit was infused with the soul of a mischievous boy. It is set in the Lake District, and if you visit Hill Top today, you can see the $17^{th}$-century old building and beautiful landscapes depicted in the books as real scenery. The picture book was originally written for a 5-year-old boy, the son of Potter's acquaintance. The good illustrations and the wonderful content encouraged people around Potter to make it into a book, so she first self-published it, gave it to her acquaintances and friends as a Christmas present, and also sold a small number of copies of the book by herself. It was published by a publisher (1902), and a year later, in 1903, more than 50,000 copies were printed and sold, making her a bestselling author. Potter was married twice, at the age of 39 (the son of a publisher) and at the age of 47 (a lawyer who collaborated with her conservation movement of nature). In her later years, she lived in the Lake District, ran a farm, worked to preserve its nature, and supported the work of the National Trust. After her death, all of her vast tracts of land in the Lake District were donated to the National Trust.

# 17. A Brief History of Scotland

Edinburgh Castle

It has been inhabited by the Celts since the 10th century BC, and they were called Picts because they had tattoos on their bodies and it looked like a painted (*pic*tured) body. The Romans called the country "Caledonia" (derived from the Caledonians, one of the groups of Picts). Scotland resisted thoroughly and was not invaded by the Roman army. Therefore, during the reign of Emperor Hadrian, Hadrian's Wall was built on the border not to be attacked by the Picts. Later, the Antonine Wall was also built. In the 8th century, the Vikings raided Scotland seriously. The Kingdom of Scotland was established in the 9th century. "Scot" was originally the name of one of the Irish tribes (Scots), so the name of the country meant "land of the Scots." After the Norman Conquest, Scotland was constantly invaded by England, but it was not controlled and remained independent. Its independence was decisive with the victory at the Battle of Bannockburn (1314). The battle was led by King Robert I of Scotland (known as Robert de Bruce), who is the most popular of the Scottish kings of all time and is highly regarded as a Scottish hero along with William Wallace. In 1513, James IV was killed at the Battle of Flodden Field. In this battle, King Henry VIII of England dealt a heavy

King Robert I

blow to the Kingdom of Scotland, and Scotland continued to decline completely thereafter.

James IV was killed in battle at the age of 40, and his son (only 1 year and 5 months old) was crowned at Stirling Castle as King James V. However, while resisting the pressure of Henry VIII of England to reform to Protestantism, James fell ill and died at the age of 30. As a result, his newborn daughter Mary Stuart at Linlithgow Castle became queen at the age of 6 days (just after six days after birth). Mary later became Queen of France, but when Francis II died at the age of 16, she returned to Scotland. The country became even more turbulent; in addition, the succession to the throne of England became involved, and Mary was executed at the age of 44 by order of Queen Elizabeth I of England. Queen Mary's son succeeded to the throne at the age of just 1 year (during his mother's lifetime), becoming King James VI of Scotland in 1567. In 1603, when King James VI also became King James I of England in the Union of the Crowns, relations between the two countries became increasingly suspicious. In 1707, Scotland joined with England by the Acts of Union. Thereafter, Scottish independence was lost. It became just the northern part of the Kingdom of Great Britain. After that, there were two large-scale rebellions (the Jacobite Risings of

William Wallace

Queen Mary I

King James VI

1715 and 1745) aimed at Scottish independence, but they were suppressed by the British army. The hero of this time was Charles Edward Stuart (1720-88), better known as Bonnie Prince Charlie, who, like his father James Francis Edward Stuart, claimed the throne of England and Scotland and revolted. He defeated the British army for a time, but eventually he got defeated and fled to the continent, where he died (in Rome). In the two world wars, Scottish soldiers are known for their bravery. In 1999, the Scottish Parliament was re-established. In 2014, a referendum on Scottish independence was held, which was narrowly rejected (44.7% in favor). Geographically, it is mainly divided into the Highlands and the Lowlands, which are culturally different and have very different temperaments of the people who live there. The tartan kilt was originally the Highlands' culture but was banned after two Jacobite risings. However, when King George IV visited Scotland in 1822, he wore a kilt, and since then it has spread throughout Scotland.

Lowlanders, many of whom were of Anglo-Saxon descent, were familiar with England and converted to Protestantism during the Reformation. Most Scottish people originally spoke Celtic (Scottish Gaelic). During the reign of Malcolm III (1031-93) Gaelic ended its role as an official language of Scotland.

However, it continued to be used in the Highlands until the 16th century and then declined. Also, there is a language called Scots (Scottish), which belongs to the Germanic language and originated in Old English. It was used mainly in the Lowlands. The Scottish Standard English appeared after the 17th century. This is undoubtedly due to the fact that King James VI of Scotland became King James I of England in 1603. This fact had a great influence on the language spoken in Scotland.

Bonnie Prince Charlie

In Scotland, the words such as *Mac*, *Mc*, *M'* are sometimes prefixed to surnames. Their meaning is *son of* or *descendant of*. Examples include MacArthur, Macbeth, MacGregor, MacKenzie, MacLean, MacMillan, and McDonald. They were originally used in the families of nobles and large landowners, but later came to be used by ordinary people as well. From around the 12th century, they came to be used as one of the ordinary surnames. The surname *Jones* is common in Scotland, and the *-s*

King George IV

ending is thought to mean Jone's *son*. Tony Blair, who served as Prime Minister of the UK from 1997 to 2007, was born in Edinburgh. *Blair* is one of the popular place names in Scotland. It means *flat land*. Other typical place names used are: *Aber* (estuary), *Dun* (hill, fort), *Eilean* (Island), *Glen* (valley), and *Loch* (lake). The capital is Edinburgh, and the largest city is Glasgow. Many Scottish writers such as Walter Scott, Conan Doyle, R. S. Steveson, and J. M. Barrie, have been born in Scotland. Additionally, many engineers and inventors, who invented the telephone, steam locomotive, and television, have also come from Scotland. The land is also the birthplace of golf, but soccer and rugby are very popular sports. It's the production area of Scotch Whisky and is famous for its food, such as haggis. Many Scottish immigrants have emigrated to the United States, Canada, Australia, and New Zealand.

Scottish men wearing tartan kilts and playing bagpipes

# 18. David Hume: The Bundle Theory of Mind

David Hume

David Hume (1711-76) was born in Edinburgh, the capital of Scotland, as the second son of Joseph Home (Hume), a lawyer and the 10$^{th}$ branch of the Earl of Home family. He lost his father when he was two years old. He entered the University of Edinburgh at the age of 11 to study law but dropped out. Later, living at his family home in Berwickshire, Scotland, he immersed himself in philosophical studies. Although Hume himself did not profess to be an atheist, he missed out on professorships at the University of Edinburgh and the University of Glasgow because he was considered an atheist. He served as a tutor to the children of nobles, military aide-de-camp, and librarian (at the University of Edinburgh) and later held positions such as secretary to the French ambassador, British chargé d'affaires, and Under Secretary of State for the Northern Department. He criticized Descartes and was the first philosopher to express skepticism about God. He also denied innate ideas. He was a hardcore skeptic and an atheist. Hume was an opinion leader of Britain's empiricists, along with Bacon and Locke, and it can be said that British empiricism was perfected by him.

Descartes' "Cogito Ergo Sum" made epistemology the central problem of modern philosophy, and from then on, rational theory became mainstream. But modern philosophy later divided into two groups. One is the continental rationalism begun with Descartes, which regards reason as absolute, later divided into German idealism and French materialism. The other is English empiricism that emphasizes experience while acknowledging human imperfections with Hume as the perfector. The former is a method of drawing a conclusion according to a certain logical or mathematical rule, such as, if "A = B" and "B = C", then "A = C", or a method of drawing another new conclusion starting from some premise (deduction). The latter is a method of finding common concepts from many observations and drawing provisional conclusions (induction).

Empiricism is the position that correct knowledge can be obtained from information, that is, experience, which has originally entered through the five human senses. The founder of empiricism was the English philosopher Bacon, born in 1561 before Descartes, and he valued experience more than logical thinking such as rational theory. Bacon's thought was succeeded by subsequent generations, such as an English philosopher John Locke (1632-1704), an Irish philosopher George Berkeley (1685-1753), and David Hume, the Scotsman. Locke argued that the mind at birth is like a blank slate *tabula rasa* with no knowledge and that our knowledge comes from observation and experience. Locke denied the existence of innate ideas. Locke's empiricism was closer to idealism in terms of methodological attitudes because it sought to show the structure of recognition through the exploration of the ideas that consciousness creates on the basis of experience. Hume's thought also inherits this attitude of Locke. But Hume strongly criticized metaphysics.

For my part, when I enter most intimately into what I call myself, I always stumble on some particular perception or other, of heat or cold, light or shade, love or hatred, pain or pleasure, I never can catch myself at any time without a perception, and never can observe any thing but perception. When my perceptions are removed for any time, as by sound sleep; so long am I insensible of myself, and may truly be said not to exist. And were all my perceptions removed by death, and could I neither think, nor feel, nor see, nor love, nor hate after the dissolution of my body…I may venture to affirm of the rest of mankind, that they are nothing but a bundle or collection of different perceptions, which succeed each other with an inconceivable rapidity, and are in perpetual flux and movement.[18]

*A Treatise of Human Nature*

Berkeley explained that to exist is to be perceived. In other words, everything in this world can be perceived not because it exists, but because it is perceived; therefore, it comes into existence. He denied the existence of material substance and insisted that familiar objects like books and pencils are ideas perceived by the human mind and cannot exist without being perceived. Everything around us, clothes, food, buildings, plants, rivers, mountains, the sun, the moon, etc., does not exist independently there. Existence refers to the perception by which someone sees or hears anything. He also argued that there is no such thing as something that is not perceived by all human beings in the world, but rather that it exists because God perceives it. This is an idea that has become extreme because of the emphasis on experience. Then Hume came along, insisting that the mind itself is simply "a bundle of perceptions." In other words, there is not even the human mind that Berkeley admitted. Hume believed that there was no substance in the world but only perception. He argued that the human mind, as well as Descartes' self in "Cogito Ergo Sum," consists of nothing more than a bundle of knowledge and perception received from experience and has no substance. This is called Bundle Theory.

> All the perceptions of the human mind resolve themselves into two distinct kinds, which I shall call IMPRESSIONS and IDEAS. The difference betwixt these consists in the degrees of force and liveliness, with which they strike upon the mind, and make their way into our thought or consciousness. Those perceptions, which enter with most force and violence, we may name impressions: and under this name I comprehend all our sensations, passions and emotions, as they make their first appearance in the soul.[19]

*A Treatise of Human Nature*

Hume held that passions rather than reason govern human behavior. Hume argued that we experience only a bundle of sensations, and the self is nothing more than this bundle of causally connected perceptions. The philosopher who said, "Man is a bundle of perceptions," insisted that perception (all that appears in the mind) is divided into two: impressions and ideas. And he thought all ideas were born from impressions, and impressions were the cause and ideas were the result. There are simple and complex, respectively. The human mind is made up of overlapping experiences, and that knowledge is formed by the combined ideas.

Hume remained skeptical of trust in reason. He held that concepts that do not exist in reality, that is, the products of the imagination, are all combinations of past experiences. Expectancy of the future is just based on past experience. Hume considered even God to be a concept created from a combination of multiple experiences.

It is therefore by EXPERIENCE only, that we can infer the existence of one object from that of another. The nature of experience is this. We remember to have had frequent instances of the existence of one species of object; and also remember, that the individuals of another species of objects have always attended them, and have existed in a regular order of contiguity and succession with regard to them. Thus we remember, to have seen that species of object we call flame, and to have felt that species of sensation we call heat. We likewise call to mind their constant conjunction in all past instances. Without any farther ceremony, we call the one cause and the other effect, and infer the existence of the one from that of the other. In all those instances, from which we learn the conjunction of particular causes and effects, both the causes and effects have been perceived by the senses, and are remembered. But in all cases, wherein we reason concerning them, there is only one perceived or remembered, and the other is supplied in conformity to our past experience.[20]

*A Treatise of Human Nature*

Hume asserts that people can only infer one object from another through experience. For example, "when approaching the flame, it is hot" is not caused by the temperature of the flame, but the experience of "approaching the fire" and feeling "it is hot" occurs one after another, and when it overlaps, people expect heat just by looking at the flame. In other words, causality means that one is perceived or remembered, and the other is supplemented to coincide with past experiences.

Hume's thought follows the theory of ideas in epistemology and belongs to the lineage of idealism that follows a German philosopher, Georg Wilhelm Friedrich Hegel (1770-1831). Hume was opposed to materialism. After all, Hume's philosophy influenced not only analytic philosophy, which has been the mainstream in the English-speaking world since the 20th century, but also continental philosophy, which has been the mainstream since the 19th century, especially a German philosopher, Immanuel Kant (1724-1804).

Hume published a number of books, including *A Treatise of Human Nature* (1739-40), *Political Discourses* (1752), and *The History of England* (1755-62). He died in Edinburgh at the age of 65 from abdominal cancer. He remained an atheist throughout his life.

Edinburgh in the 1990s

# 19. **Walter Scott:** The man who believed in the progress of human history

## Medievalism

Sir Walter Scott, 1st Baronet (1771-1832) was a poet and historian from Edinburgh, Scotland, who later became the most popular historical novelist in Europe and one of Scotland's greatest historical figures. During his time as a writer, Scott worked as Sheriff-Depute of Selkirkshire and as Clerk of Session (a clerk of the Supreme Courts of Scotland). He became a baronet of Abbotsford in 1820, and he was a socially responsible person throughout his life.

In Britain, the 19th century was a savage and dangerous age, despite the extreme economic prosperity. In these difficult situations, some people came to feel nostalgia for the past. The life style and social system of the past, especially the medieval times, became an example of life. Chivalry was again accepted as a model in this confused

Sir Walter Scott

society. In the Middle Ages, religious people believed in many miracles of God, having fertile imagination. Feudal lords looked after the poor just like their parents, since all classes were linked together. The lower class was under the protection of the ruling class, wherein medieval Catholic churches gave the wealth of the rich to the poor. The Middle Ages were full of love and philanthropy.

Some came to think that people in the Middle Ages had been much happier than their contemporaries; others thought that they should recur to their former Ages, which might stop the collapse of the society. For them, the restoration of medievalism was the best way to clear the contradiction so that they could maintain public order. Meanwhile, Britain as a nation grew up larger and stronger. It raised the patriotic spirit of the British people. With their economic success, the country grew up as one of the top-ranking nations in Europe, which let them feel nationalism. This is the time when British people would look back to the old Celtic world and the exciting Anglo-Saxon history. The reason why Celtic and Anglo-Saxon cultures received much attention was, not only that they were quite different from Norman culture, but also, they were different from the 18$^{th}$ century classicism idealizing the Greek and Roman civilization. The people in the 19$^{th}$ century in Britain yearned after their own original culture that was unsophisticated

but never untouched by other cultures. Returning to the past, some people tried to have vivid medieval experience in order to spread the range of vision to judge the unknown society controlled over by science and machinery. They came to think that medieval knights were primitive, brilliant, and broad-

Abbotsford House

minded. They thought that medieval people should be praised, and words, such as "Gothic" or "grotesque," which only had negative meanings before, now came to have an affirmative meaning. Ancient legends and ballads were gradually received and recognized. At this moment, Walter Scott appeared. Scott devoted himself exclusively to the past of Scotland. He regarded himself as a minstrel of his time and he was obsessed with leaving many poems and epics. Then, he became a novelist, writing twenty-seven historical novels

Sir Walter Scott

including *Waverley* (1814), *Guy Mannering* (1815), *The Antiquary* (1816), *Rob Roy* (1817), *The Heart of Mid-Lothian* (1818), *Ivanhoe* (1819), *The Abbot* (1820), and *Kenilworth* (1821). Scott was sometimes said to be a medievalist. However, he was also aware of the boundaries of the time. He knew the uncivilized aspect of the medieval world. He did not seem to wish for the past to come back. The idea that Scott really wanted to say is not the same as the stereotypical medieval image.

Scotland was a country that had collapsed and merged into Great Britain. Scott believed that it was the progress of history. What is in the base of his works is that Scott always tried to find some kind of order in history. Considering the radical history of Scotland, Scott became totally a gradualist, and hated radicalism. He was not an anachronism but a reformist. This kind of personality was necessary for Scotland at that time. He once again made the Scots, who had lost confidence, proud of their lost homeland. He asked the English to understand Scotland. He admitted the reality and tried to cultivate Scotland which had been

Ellen's Isle on Loch Katrine

always too chaotic and unstable. Some critics said that Scott was too submissive to the English government. But, his personality as a moderate was necessary, and his wholesomeness was what Scotland really needed at that time. That brought King George IV to Scotland in 1822, and made Queen Victoria favor Highlanders, building Balmoral Castle in Scotland in 1853. Here we can find Scott's attitude to include all different ideas to unite. We assert that his view of history is a fusion towards the good.

Scott's sense for the medieval had two sides. On the one hand, as nostalgic people and the medieval lovers say, Scott felt that a society based on chivalry was better than a society based on commercialism. On the other hand, Scott knew the uncivilized aspect of the era of knights, and he did not seem to wish for the medieval to come back as the medievalists wanted to. Scott did not criticize the modern society by making the medieval a model. Scott affirmed the sympathy and generosity of knighthood but he denied the attitude of chivalry focused on fame and power. Scott instinctively felt that the medieval society had immeasurable power hidden, which would give its stronghold of life to modern fragile daily life. But he did not seek for the ideal in the Middle Ages. He just borrowed themes from the medieval romances to seek out how he could save the people in the 19th century. While he stuck to the past, Scott also believed in the progress of the society. His father was a lawyer and Scott also became one. What he hated most was a disorder or chaos. To develop an idealistic society, he thought it was necessary to have legal procedures.

## The Message of *The Lady of the Lake*

It was Scott's will that in *The Lady of the Lake*, Ellen did not prefer to be radical, so that she refused to marry Roderick, chieftain of the Highlands. Scott did not like an extreme violence and he denied people who were too brave. Undoubtedly, the real protagonist of *The Lady of the Lake* is not King James V, but Ellen's father, James Douglas, who is banished from the royal palace of Stirling Castle for a gratuitous plot, endures suffering, and in the end, his honor is restored. Exploring the actions and statements of the old knight Douglas suggests an answer to the question of what Scott really meant of "honor." The figure of Douglas symbolizes not taking credit in battle, but rather living positively in the midst of failure and hardship, not despairing, and persevering with faith in the nation. Even though the environment in which he lives has changed and the outside world has changed drastically, Douglas's inner core is solid, and he never forgets his honor, and he bears the trials imposed on him and lives with strength in the real world. Douglas prides himself on having unwavering virtue, and Scott believed that such a way of life was a truly

Ellen and her father Douglas met King James V

honorable way of life. The regulation of war by chivalry eventually pushed war to become a sport, and "sport" was passed down from generation to generation as a gentleman's pastime. Hunting also seems to have been necessary for the development of a chivalrous spirit, and Douglas avoided fighting against King James and passed his moderate time by going hunting. The knights who appear in the story have romantic feelings for Ellen, the beauty of the lake, and the story revolves around her, but Douglas is Ellen's

King James V

father, and his feeling for her is family love. Douglas's love for his family translates into patriotism for his society, and Douglas is portrayed as a selfless person who is loyal to his country. Douglas, who believes in the goodness of the king (=state) and endures his current situation, was once the king's guardian, and his feelings of admiration for the king who exiled him do not change. In order to avoid a decisive battle with the king and save his friends Roderick and Malcolm, Douglas goes to the royal castle, Stirling, alone, and eventually he is captured and imprisoned by the guards. When it is discovered that the man is Douglas, the people of the castle town riot against the king. Douglas addresses the people to stop the riots. Douglas, who has reached old age, has a strong belief in the observance of order, and even if he is treated unfairly by the king, he does not rise up and keeps on enduring. He feels deep sorrow for the people who are revolting to save him, and he decides to entrust his life to the king. This attitude of Douglas is similar to that of the Duke of Argyll in *The Heart of Mid-Lothian* when he suppressed the Jacobite rebellion. Burning with anger, not respecting public stability and well-being, obsessed with revenge and victory, is not true courage or honor. Disrespecting the law is not what Scott wanted as a lawyer. The important thing is not to expand one's own desires and ambitions. In any situation, we must have the courage to stop making easy and hasty decisions and actions, and to seek a peaceful solution. Scott created Douglas as the embodiment of the ideal chivalry. With this narrative poem, Scott wanted to convey to his contemporaries, the Scottish people of his time, what true courage is.

"Without courage," he said, "there cannot be truth;
and without truth there can be no other virtue."[21]

### Neo-Chivalry

All the introductory epistles of *Marmion* are pipelines between fiction and non-fiction. Also, to list many historical facts made people realize that history is alive and still going on. Many memorable words in Scottish history are used very often in *Marmion*. Scott thought that he must leave Scottish history in some way or other. These are the reasons why he stuck to the things that had changed or vanished, and also times,

Stirling Castle

places, and proper nouns were very important factors for his works. Scott passionately restored the medieval world of Scotland in the period of enlightenment. The Lowlands were on the English side, and Scott, one of the Lowlanders, was basically on the English side. Yet, he also had feelings towards the Highlanders. He wanted to find romanticism in the Scottish Highlands. According to the modern history of Britain, many Highland soldiers died in the war when the British Empire extended its colonies. Many Highlanders were sent to new colonies overseas; others lost their lands when the Highland Clearances were put into operation. In spite of these cruel treatments from the British government, the Highlanders never lost their honor and pride. What stopped riots from breaking out in Scotland might have been due to Scott's contribution. Scott always protected them, supported them, and instructed them on how to behave. In *Waverley*, Scott says:

> ...and that he[Edward Waverley] felt himself entitled to say firmly, though perhaps with a sigh, that the romance of his life was ended, and that its real history had now commenced. [22]

Tantallon Castle

This excerpt can be interpreted as his message for Scotland, that the medieval world had ended. Scott showed the glorious past of Scotland to encourage Scottish people to take pride in them. However, one should not always stick to one's past. What Scott meant in this part is to make progress by facing reality. History is the gradual change of time towards harmony, and although the paths are full of trials and tribulations, it is so fair with a sense of neo-chivalry. I remember that when I was invited to visit a Scottish family, the bookshelves in the study were often lined with the complete works of Scott alongside the Bible. It was just like the complete works of Shakespeare in the study of an English home with the Bible.

## General Principles of History

J. G. Lockhart (1794-1854) was Scott's son-in-law and the literary critic who understood Scott best, both publicly and privately. His biography *Memoirs of the Life of Sir Walter Scott* (1837-38), which is the basis of Scott studies, begins with a quotation from Scott's autobiography. It is a long sentence that recalls Scott's own reading experience in his youth.

...but I gradually assembled much of what was striking and picturesque in historical narrative; and when, in riper years, I attended more to the deduction of general principles, I was furnished with a powerful host of examples in illustration of them. [emphasis added][23]

The "general principles" mentioned here would later become Scott's motifs of historical works. What exactly are the "general principles" of making history that Scott envisioned? In general, Scott's epics and vast collection of historical novels often depict

Linlithgow Castle 1

Linlithgow Castle 2

landscapes and historical facts in detail with innovative angles and rich storylines, but rarely deal with philosophical descriptions nor consciousness of the characters. Many of them contain little or no description of the author's personal views, thoughts, or philosophical beliefs. Therefore, the specific content of principles of making history is also somewhat difficult to find traces of, compared to the Romantic poet Wordsworth (1770-1850). For Scott, a very successful novelist, historical fiction is all about a plot that entertains readers, and it seems that it is enough to depict what the characters said and what they did. Therefore, it is not easy to derive Scott's principles of history immediately from his works. However, this is an extremely important research topic, and I would like to look at Scott's works, letters, diaries, and critical biographies written by his contemporaries, and reconsider what principles of history Scott deduced.

Linlithgow Castle 3

## Stranger is a Holy Name

There is a scene in the narrative poem, *The Lady of the Lake* where the Highlander knight Roderick encounters the lost and exhausted Lowlander knight Fitz-James, and Roderick says, "To assail a wearied man were shame, / And stranger is a holy name."[24] For Scott, the gothic, the grotesque, and the incomprehensible were not objects of disgust or fear, but rather he tended to acknowledge their existence and treat them with favor and accept them despite their danger. Scott was even conscious of actively entering into them at times. As a result, he expanded and revitalized

The Old Tolbooth, Edinburgh

himself. Of course, this also ties into the spirit of the adventurous medieval knight, a trait shared by Scott's many characters. In 1817, Scott told the American writer Washington Irving (1783-1858), who visited Abbotsford House, about a strange painting on the wall of the Abbotsford House.[25] The episode of the painting is about a young English knight captured near the border, locked in the dungeon of the castle, forced to be hanged on the gallows or marry the ugly daughter (called "Ugly Meg") of the lord of the castle, whose mouth is torn from her ears. The English

knight finally decides to get married to Ugly Meg because of his attachment to life. However, contrary to most people's expectations, the marriage turned out to be a very happy one. This story can be interpreted as a result of human diversity, but there is also an attitude of accepting the strange or the grotesque and growing oneself. And this would be one of the principles that would make the history that Scott envisioned. This is because it can be said that the history of Britain itself was a history built on the influx of various races (strangers) and the

Jeanie Deans at Reuben Butler's home

conflict and reconciliation with the natives. It is natural that Scott had this view of history. Marmion, the English knight of *Marmion: A Tale of Flodden Field* (1808), is a stranger to the Scots, and similarly, Captain Edward Waverley, the protagonist of *Waverley; or, 'Tis Sixty Years Since* (1814), is a stranger to the Scots, and it is easy to imagine that the heroine of *The Heart of Mid-Lothian* (1818), Jeanie Deans, is also a stranger to the English. Regardless of who the person is, the attitude of opening one's heart is Scott's principle. Scott's open-mindedness and acceptance of others, without discrimination, gives rise to the perspective that, as the following quote says, "From the lips of the poor and uneducated we sometimes hear opinions more advanced than the Bible."

> I [Scott] have read books enough, and observed and conversed with enough of eminent and splendidly cultivated minds, too, in my time; but, I assure you, I have heard higher sentiments from the lips of poor uneducated men and women, when exerting the spirit of severe yet gentle heroism under difficulties and affections, or speaking their simple thoughts as to circumstances in the lot of friends and neighbours, than I ever yet met with out of the pages of the Bible. [26]

Effie (left) and Jeanie Deans (right)

The meaning of 'Stranger is a holy name' is an attitude to welcome a "stranger" who may even threaten the other person's life with fear and a little anticipation. By doing so, new values are shared, the world around you expands, and a better society will be

Duke of Argyle

born with new vitality. On the other hand, we should be more aware that "strangers" should also have the courage to venture into the unknown world, as well as sufficient abilities, charms, and diverse qualities to be accepted by others.

## Honor and Self-Respect

I would like to mention the honor and self-respect that are common concepts to the main characters in Scott's works. For example, the Duke of Argyle in *The Heart of Mid-lothian* is portrayed as a good leader to the Scottish people and as a fair politician, who is Scott's ideal. The way the Duke of Argyle treats himself in moderation, his presence, and his influence on the Scots make him a favorite of Scott. As a Scottish aristocratic statesman, the Duke of Argyle always acted with the utmost honor, and earned the immense trust of the people of his homeland. In 1715, when the Highlanders rallied and invaded England, the Duke led his private army to stop the rebels on behalf of the Hanoverian royal family in London. And when the riot was over, he helped the Scottish nobles who got involved in the incident because of their false patriotism. On the other hand, in the British Parliament, he freely voiced critical opinions to the royal family, and as a result, he was seen by the royal family and ministers as a powerful and dangerous member of

Argyll's Lodging situated below Stirling Castle

Parliament. The cause of the dispute in Parliament was usually Scottish matters, which made the Duke of Argyle more and more popular, and the Scots respected and adored him. In his work, Scott praises the Duke as a very honorable man.[27] And Scott told through the Duke that it was important for everyone to have pride or self-respect, and that the Duke's self-respect was definitely a respect for the people of his native country, Scotland.

## Spirit of Tolerance

Next, I would like to consider the spirit of tolerance. Jeffrey (1773-1850) had long been Scott's fellow lawyer, but he had been in rivalry with Scott both literarily and politically. Scott appreciated and admired the brilliant Jeffrey, but in a letter to the playwright Joanna Baillie (1762-1851), Scott made a harsh comment on Jeffrey. In response to the suggestion that a tribute to Jeffrey should be sent in Scott's work, Scott said that it was not a good idea with a little excitement.[28] According to Scott, what Jeffrey lacks is a macroscopic eye, an aesthetic eye that finds the good points of other persons rather than their weaknesses. He is short of the kindness that alleviates the flaws of the people. Jeffrey's heart needs to accept human weakness and frailty. Washington Irving, who was welcomed and stayed at Abbotsford for a while, described Scott's interaction with the villagers and workers at the mansion.

> ...he [Scott] looked upon poor human nature with an indulgent eye, relishing what was good and pleasant, tolerating what was frail, and pitying what was evil.[29]

We can see how Scott acknowledged diversity and treated people with acceptance, which was his attitude towards the weak and evil. Those around him often forgot that Scott was a major figure in the Scottish legal profession and one of the greatest and most popular writers in Europe at the time. Scott spoke so intimately with people from all walks of life. Scott always listened and understood, no matter how insignificant the opponent's status or claims were. There was no contempt or ridicule in Scott's conversations, but a sense of humor. The belief that "no human life can appear otherwise than weak and filthy in the eyes of God"[30] was deeply rooted in his psyche. There is no doubt that Scott valued the spirit of tolerance for human folly above all else. His attitude was accurately expressed in the review of Scott's *The Works of Jonathan Swift* (1814-) in the *Edinburgh Review*.

...the good sense and toleration of a man of the world, with much of that generous allowance for the 'Fears of the brave and follies of the wise,'[31]

"The fear of the brave and the folly of the wise" describes Scott's eye for all human beings who have ever been born into this world. The recognition that not only celebrities but also historical heroes and heroines are not immune to that sort of failing, is common to many of characters in Scott's work. As a result, even diabolical dark heroes such as Roderick (the chief of Clan Alpine in *The Lady of the Lake*) and Fergus Mac-Ivor (a Highland chieftain, in *Waverley*), as well as Marmion and Richard Varney (in *Kenilworth*), were treated as someone who can be forgiven. Scott, as a fellow human being, felt sorry for their wickedness. The reader, too, becomes less angry with them, and feels a pity for them. The more we are exposed to historical figures, the more we realize how helpless and foolish human beings are. Scott was fond of saying: "The wisest of our race often reserves the average stock of folly to be all expended upon some one flagrant absurdity."[32] In fact, Scott himself had made a big mistake in his life. He kept it a secret even from many of his closest friends, but the truth is that Scott got involved in running a publisher (Archibald Constable and co.) that eventually went bankrupt. Thereafter, Scott continued to write and devote himself to paying off his debts even after he suffered a stroke. Scott himself reluctantly became the embodiment of the follies of the wise. However, in spite of these harsh realities, Scott wrote in his diary of May 6, 1826:

'Are these things then necessities?
Then let us meet them like necessities.'

*King Henry VI.* Act III. Scene 1.[33]

In a sense, it can be said that human history has been supported by a strong spirit of "tolerance" such as "if it is inevitable, let's accept it as inevitable." A generous spirit that softens our shortcomings empowers us to repent our mistakes, to overcome our weaknesses, and to free ourselves from what is truly wicked. This spirit of tolerance can also be a major pillar of the principles that make history.

## Sad Story of Humanity

Next, I will refer to Scott's pessimistic view of history. Scott is said to have longed to write a biography of Alexander Pope (1688-1744) after writing *Life of Jonathan Swift.*[34] Naturally, Scott must have been influenced by Pope's works. *An Essay on Man* (1733-34) has the theme of "Whatever Is is right," and Scott's principles of history are not necessarily off the mark. In his works, too, the destination of opposing concepts such as friends and foes, good and evil, is reconciliation, and it is characteristic of Scott's work that he depicted historical events from a very impartial perspective. Scott knew that the conflict between individuals and groups is highly accidental, and that it is futile to hate each other and take revenge on each other. Even so, tragedies are piled up on top of each other, and this is the folly of human beings and the sorrow of human history. The disappointment with the progress of history often becomes a romantic sentimentality for what has been lost for Scott in his works. In real life, however, Scott was a very pragmatic man, always affirming the union of Scotland and England. Scott maintained a balanced gradualist position in favor of a union with England. Fully aware of the glories and sorrows of Scottish history, he affirmed the gradual promotion of two countries while preserving Scottish traditions and culture as much as possible. Those that existed in this world, no matter how outrageous and tragic they were, humbly accepted the fact and tried to find some meaning. In addition, Scott tried to understand and evaluate the significance of things that actually exist as much as possible. This perspective is very similar to the spirit of "Whatever Is is right" (=Everything is fair that exists in this world). Not all of the history-makers, heroes, and heroines will live the life they want to live. How often do virtuous people meet tragic ends? There are many people who live and die at the mercy of "fate" beyond

Alexander Pope

Kenilworth Castle

human comprehension. Scott depicted many people who disappeared due to the great swells of history that were beyond the control of human beings. "Not you, but Fate, has vanquish'd me"[35], the Duchess of Buccleuch excuses Cranstoun in *The Lay of the Last Minstrel.* Similarly, Bonnie Prince Charlie, the young prince portrayed in *Waverley*, who challenged the Hanoverians with the help of the Jacobites (Stuart royalists), is also a tragic protagonist at the mercy of fate. Amy, the tragic heroine of *Kenilworth; A Romance.* is also forced to keep her marriage a secret for her husband, Robert Dudley, Earl of Leicester, who has gained power and honor in the favor of Queen Elizabeth I, and in the end, she dies (It is based on the historical fact that her husband, the Earl of Leicester, is suspected of killing his wife in order to marry Queen Elizabeth). Constance de Beverly, the unfortunate nun who was killed by the sinful English knight Marmion, is also the heroine of a tragedy. And *Wandering Willie's Tale* (1824) features Steenie Steenson, the protagonist whose fate is at the mercy of the ghost of Sir Robert Redgauntlet. Other historical figures appear in *Tales of Grandfather* (1827) and *History of Scotland* (1829), such as Queen of Scots, Mary (who was killed by Queen Elizabeth), Macbeth (King of Scotland), James IV (killed in the Battle of Flodden), and William Wallace and Robert Bruce (both contributed to the independence of Scotland). They all put their fate in the hands of history and were all manipulated, whether they wanted it or not. Scott said, "No eyes the rocks discover, which lurk beneath the deep"[36] or "After all, one can does what one can"[37] in a letter to Joanna Baillie (1762-1851). In other words, there is a limit to what people can know and do, and no one can know or understand the future. Faced with the bankruptcy of a publishing company in which he had a major role in its management, heavy debts, and the dying illness of his beloved wife, Charlotte, Scott wrote in his diary on December 18, 1825.

"What a life mine has been! — half educated, almost wholly neglected, or left to myself; stuffing my head with most nonsensical trash, and undervalued by most of my companions for a time; ...But what is to be the end of it? God knows; and so ends the catechism..."[38]

Scott, who has suffered a series of misfortunes in real life, has a very pessimistic view of history. And, as David Daiches[39] and Edwin Muir[40] point out, Scott ultimately believed that the course of history was beyond the reach of human will. "To let the tree lie as it had fallen"[41], The idea is that even if you remove the fallen giant tree, even if you wake it up, there is no change in your fate, and whether you take any major action or not, there is not much difference from the great flow of history, but it is just a repetition of happiness and misfortune. Scott tried to accept reality as it is, as much as possible, as a fact based on the past, and to affirm everything that exists. However, he was cautious about making changes that were too hasty.

"Leave him to God, who punishes the wicked in his time;"[42]

When Scott created his literary works, he showed great attention to detail, depicting the era in which the work is set. The entire work is composed of an accumulation of detailed depictions, and everything that existed, from the serfs to the princes and aristocrats who lived in that era and region, is depicted vividly and on a grand scale. There was a viewpoint that sought out the facts as accurately as possible, and there was an unbiased perspective that pursued historical truth. In particular, he paid attention to the details of the customs and habits of the people who lived in that era. He depicted human activities that were always beyond the human power. He depicted the human figure of a small being who was tossed around in the great flow of history. He depicted the tragic consequences of a human being, first, shortsightedly, second, at eye level, and then, on a grand scale, corrected, adjusted, and supported by the great flow of history. He hated ethnic prejudices and people who were driven by misguided patriotism to commit reckless and cruel acts. He revived the grief of the Highlanders, the Boarders, and the English knights who lived in a radical and violent medieval world with no order. At the same time, it is worth mentioning that Scott also had a positive and optimistic view of history, in which what seems to be the worst is not so fatal, showing that he is not a complete pessimist. The following quote illustrates Scott's idea:

The bad is not always so very bad, and the good is not always so very good. [43]

Scott also faced the hardships that befell him, risking his life. It overlaps with the image of James Douglas or the Duke of Argyle. Scott's passion for confronting his turbulent fate was supported by a heart that cherished honor. De Wilton in *Marmion* is at the mercy of fate, deprived of his title and estate, and even in the depths of despair, he endures every day with a positive attitude without the slightest hesitation in his love and faith. His honor is preserved and finally restored. He happily marries his lover, Clare. Henry of Cranstoun, the proud knight in *The Lay of the Last Minstrel*, is devoted to his enemy, the Duchess of Buccleuch, and is allowed to marry her daughter Margaret. Edmund Tressilian in *Kenilworth* is also treated as a madman by Queen Elizabeth, but he still defends his honor to the end. In *The Lady of the Lake*, King James reconciles and restores Douglas honor in front of his servants in the Great Hall of Stirling Castle in the end. This kind of ending can be said to be the result of Scott's sense of balance, isn't it?

## Human History Moving Towards Good

In the history of nations flourishing and perishing, do people have no choice but to live as they are? Scott, who had an optimistic side, had a positive view of history, that the passage of time was progress and good. Or he had a fusion view of history in which the unknown, the strange, and the grotesque were absorbed and developed more and more within themselves. However, the reality is that there are severe conflicts everywhere, and people die in the midst of hardship. Scott concluded that in the stream of this difficult history, the only hope is for people to accept others, to forgive the shortcomings of others with a spirit of tolerance, to remember a sense of honor and self-respect, and to face difficulties with courage. This is none other than Scott's own way of life. It was Scott's unbridled sense of honor that created his self-esteem and his strong sense of responsibility to society.[44] Referring to the Battle of Flodden (1513), which symbolized Scotland's eternal defeat against England, Scott insisted that the Scots should never lose their honor in his letter to Miss Seward of February 20, 1807.

...that at Flodden all was lost but our honour[45]

We are born into this world, and we often rely too much on knowledge and reason. Sometimes we are drowning in the glory of the past and dreams, and worrying about the vague anxieties of the future. However, as human beings who are involved in the changes of history in real time, we must not forget to fulfill the responsibilities and roles given to us, valuing a sense of honor above all else. True honor is one's own truth, one's true self, and all one's goodness. We will not forget the spirit of family love, compassion, and tolerance, and we will make the most of our intelligence and sensitivity to engage in society. And it is only by living life to the fullest in this way that we have the potential to turn the chaotic flow of history in the direction of universal goodness. This is the essence of what Scott sought to convey through his works.

A monument stands at the place where the Battle of Flodden was fought.

# 20. History of Germany, Part I

Germany borders Denmark to the north, facing both the North Sea and the Baltic Sea. The northern part of the country has a series of plains, where rye, potatoes, and sugar beets (raw materials for sugar) are grown. Dairy farming including raising cows and pigs, is popular on the plateau from central to south, and the southern part bordering Switzerland and Austria, has a high altitude, with the Alps running along the border. The area along the Rhine River in western Germany is an industrial area, and the southwest is covered with fir trees and other black forests (called Schwarzwald).

Today, Germany's forest covers 32% of its land, and the people of Germany love forests very much. Forests are the spiritual home of Germany, and the history of Germany began with the clearing of deep forests and creating new fields there. Originally, the Germanic people were called "forest people." The Black Forest, composed of evergreen conifers, would have cultivated the unique sense of beauty of the German people. This may explain why Gothic buildings are prominent for being constructed in large numbers in Germany.

The word "Germany" is derived from the Latin "Germania," which means "land of the "Germani." However, the etymology of "Germani" remains unknown. The Germanic peoples migrated south from the northern Baltic Sea around the $3^{rd}$ century BC, drove out the

Odoacer

indigenous Celts, and settled there. They worshiped nature and became polytheists. They raised cattle and farmed in forest glades, ate rye and butter, and drank beer. They also crossed the Rhine and Danube rivers into Gaul territory. Eventually, Caesar pushed them back and made Gaul a province of the Roman Empire. In the $1^{st}$ century, the Romans built a 550-kilometer-long earthwork known as the "Limes Germanicus" to divide the Roman Empire and the unsubdued German tribes. Some Germanic tribes remained in Roman territory and followed Rome as peasants and soldiers. One of these mercenaries, Odoacer (433-493), who became a mercenary captain and eventually a general in the Roman army, dethroned Emperor Romulus of the Western Roman Empire by force in 476. Odoacer himself became lord of Italy.

Then Germanic states were created in the territory of the former Roman Empire. One of them was the Frankish Kingdom (founded in 482). Originally, the Franks lived in the lower reaches of the Rhine, around present-day Netherlands and Belgium. Soon, their domains expanded through war, and in the late $8^{th}$ century, Charlemagne (748-814) became king of the most extensive

kingdom in Europe. Charlemagne was appointed and crowned emperor in Rome by Pope Leo III in 800. However, after the death of Charlemagne, the Frankish kingdom (768-814) was

Burg Stahleck and the Rhine

divided into three (East Francia, West Francia, and Middle Francia=Kingdom of Italy), and when Otto I (912-973) became king of East Francia (later Germany) and king of Italy, Otto was crowned as

Schloss Sigmaringen

Holy Roman Emperor (=Carolingian Empire) in 962.

The Holy Roman Empire (Heiliges Römisches Reich) was ruled by the king of Germany (the Holy Roman Emperor), and it became the largest territory in the $13^{th}$ century. Its territorial range included present-day Germany, Austria, the Czech Republic, northern Italy, and eastern France, forming a multiethnic state. In the $16^{th}$ century, during the reign of the Holy Roman Emperor Charles V, there was a conflict between Catholicism and Lutheranism (Protestantism). In the end, individual freedom of religion was not allowed, and people were allowed to decide whether they were Catholic or Protestant depending on the region or city in which they lived.

When Ferdinand II, who became Holy Roman Emperor, tried to impose religious unity on his territories (Austria, Bohemia, Hungary, etc.), the countries of northern

Schloss Harburg

Schloss Neuschwanstein

Germany formed a Protestant Union, and the Catholic countries of southern Germany formed a Catholic Union in opposition. Countries such as Sweden and France took part in the confrontation. Catholics and Protestants fought a religious war in Germany (Holy Roman Empire) from 1618 to 1648, resulting in the independence of the Netherlands and Switzerland, which were part of Spain before. France expanded its territory and became the most powerful country on the continent, while Sweden gained northern Germany. The "Holy Roman Empire" was neutralized but nominally survived until Napoleon became emperor of France in 1806 (which was still a blessing for the weaker countries because they were able to exist as independent states without being invaded by other countries). Germany suffered many casualties (8 million people, or 20% of the population, died in the war), and the country was greatly devastated and decayed (around this time, plague, cholera, typhus, and other plagues spread all over the country). This series of wars is called the "Thirty Years' War." In order to restore the devastated land, many of the territorial states pursued strong absolutism (territorial absolutism) and mercantilism.

In the Napoleonic Wars, Germany continued to lose and could not win by

Goethe

any means. Prussia also lost half of its territory, and Germany surrendered to Napoleon. During this time, Prussia succeeded in rebuilding the country through reforms. On the other hand, Austria, which remained in its old constitution, declined. Prussia allied with Russia and declared war on France when Napoleon's expedition to Russia failed. After the war, the Vienna Protocol created the new "Germany Bund" (Deutscher Bund) in 1815, consisting of 35 states (including the Austrian Empire, which held the presidency of the Bundestag, the Kingdom of Prussia, Saxony, Hanover, Bavaria, etc.) and four free cities (Hamburg, Frankfurt, etc.). In 1848, the "February Revolution" occurred in France and the "March Revolution" occurred in Germany. Then the Constitutional Diet was held, and Germany became a modern and constitutional state.

In the past, Gutenberg (1398-1468), who invented letterpress printing technology, was born in Germany. But, when we think of Germany's contribution to the world's art and science, the first thing that comes to mind is classical music represented by Bach, Beethoven (1770-1827), and Brahms, and the second, from the $19^{th}$ century onwards, is the field of natural sciences. Röntgen (1845-1923) from the Kingdom of Prussia, who won the first Nobel Prize in

Beethoven

Röntgen          Einstein

Physics, discovered X-rays and made a significant contribution to the medical community that followed. It is true that Germany is at the forefront of the world in the fields of science, medicine, pharmacy, chemistry, and physics. In addition, Japan's medical society modeled Germany's medicine on its model for a long time. Albert Einstein (1879-1955), a theoretical physicist famous for his theory of relativity, was born in the Kingdom of Württemberg.

In the world of literature, there is Goethe (1749-1832), who was born in Frankfurt. Other famous German writers are Schiller, Heine, the Brothers Grimm (who spread German folk tales to the world), Thomas Mann (Nobel Prize), and Hermann Hesse (Nobel Prize). Considering the national character of Germany, it is distinguishable that German people are diligent, serious, responsible, strict with rules, rationalistic, and prioritize reason over emotion, it is evident that they are fond of logic, which eventually leads them to get into philosophy. Kant was from Königsberg (now Kaliningrad) in Prussia, and Hegel, the leader of German idealism, was from Stuttgart in the Duchy of Württemberg. Karl Marx was born in Trier in the Kingdom of Prussia. Marx perfected the theory of socialism, which aimed to realize a society in which workers could live with peace of mind, which would have a great influence on the world situation thereafter. Germany also gave birth to important philosophers such as Schopenhauer, who preached pessimism, and Nietzsche, who declared that "God is dead."

# 21. **Kant:** Rationalism and Empiricism Complement Each Other

Immanuel Kant

Immanuel Kant was born as the fourth of nine children of a German harness maker, Johann Georg Kant, and Anna Regina Reuter, in Königsberg, the capital of East Prussia, in 1724. He entered the University of Königsberg and after leaving school, he worked as a tutor for about 9 years. Then he submitted his dissertation to the university and obtained a master's degree. Later (1770), he became a professor at the University of Königsberg (Faculty of Philosophy). Sixteen years later, he became president of the university. After all, he spent his whole career there.

Kant held that understanding and experience do not exist separately but complement each other. Intelligence can only be obtained through experience, and that intelligence is never absolute. We always understand the limits of thought. He established a philosophy that integrated Continental rationalism and British empiricism. And in the world of that time, where people believed that Christian values and morality could only be obtained by having faith, Kant insisted that anyone could obtain them. He held that Man has certain moral laws that he should follow and that if he acts according to those laws, he can be free. He believed that human intelligence has its limits, but morality is infinite. Trying to be a moral person is worthy of happiness, and it is more important than actual happiness. He always wondered, "What is cognition?" How can we perceive things correctly? In epistemology, which addresses the question of such knowledge, "To what extent is the limit of human knowledge?", philosophers were at odds between the positions of rational theory, which valued logical thinking, and empiricism, which valued experience. It was the German philosopher Kant who settled the matter. Kant criticized rational theory because when people tried to gain knowledge through logical thinking and were confronted with something beyond the limits of their own thinking power, they would think that God exists, like Descartes, in order to make sense of it. Kant criticized empiricism because if we try to obtain knowledge from experience alone, we will eventually come to the extreme conclusion that, like David

Kant

Hume, there is no matter in this world. This is because British empiricists believed that there is no such thing as matter in this world and that it does not exist because it exists, but because it is perceived. Hume said that matter is nothing more than a bundle of perceptions. For Kant, both the idea of rational theory and the idea of empiricism are necessary for correct recognition. Kant argued that human beings can gain knowledge by logical thinking in their heads based on experience.

University of Königsberg

Kant is also a philosopher who set the limits of the extent to which Man can perceive the world. First, he argued that human beings cannot know things themselves and can only know phenomena such as light and sound emitted by things. This is because, when Man sees or touches things, he recognizes objects after defining them in a way, which is easy for him to understand. For example, let's suppose you are watching TV, and you see a person in the center of the screen and a mountain in the distance. However, there are no actual people in the TV, the screen is flat, and the mountain is not really there. Yet, people watch TV as if they were real, and they have a sense of substance because they are changing the information that comes in through sight and hearing so that it is easier for them to understand. The same can be said for the scenery we see in reality. Therefore, Man cannot recognize pure things themselves. He then said that it was pointless to think about things that transcended time and space, that is, about God, the soul, the afterlife, the Idea, and so on. Since they cannot recognize their existence through the five senses, they are not within the scope of philosophy. There may or may not be God, the soul, the afterlife, or the Idea, but Kant concluded that there is no need to debate it. Descartes said that human reason is infinite, but Kant said that it is finite. Kant said that it is impossible to argue about metaphysics that is not limited by experience (or an invisible one) and that such arguments fall into Antinomie (antinomy) or a paradox. Therefore, those are not subject to treatment in philosophy but only to the object of faith. Rationalists said that the empirical is individual and not universal, but Kant pursued the universal with the knowledge gained from the experience of reality.

Kant wrote so many great, important books and articles. His most notable three critical works are *Kritik der reinen Vernunft* (*Critique of Pure Reason*, 1781; second edition 1787), *Kritik der praktischen Vernunft* (*Critique of Practical Reason*, 1788), and *Kritik der Urteilskraft* (*Critique of Judgment*, 1790). These are considered his masterpieces. As for his appearance, Kant was said to be a small man. He continued to live a very strict life. He was punctual and walked at a fixed time every day. He never married to be single all his life. He died at Königsberg in 1804, at the age of 79, uttering "*Es ist gut* (It is good)" just before death.

# 22. Hegel: Das absolute Wissen

Georg W. F. Hegel

Called the "Perfectionist of Modern Philosophy," a German philosopher, Georg Wilhelm Friedrich Hegel, was born in 1770 in the Duchy of Wörttemberg, the son of Georg Ludwig, who was an official. Hegel was the same age as Beethoven (1770-1827) and a year younger than Napoleon (1769-1821). Hegel lost his mother Maria at the age of 13. He studied theology and philosophy at the University of Tübingen and, after graduation, worked as a private tutor to a wealthy family. Then he became an unsalaried lecturer at the University of Jena (Friedrich-Schiller-Universität Jena), but the Kingdom of Prussia surrendered due to Napoleon's invasion, and Jena was occupied by French troops. The university was closed, and he lost his position. After that, he worked as an editor for a newspaper. Then he got the post of headmaster of a school. In 1816, he became a professor at the University of Heidelberg (Ruprecht-Karls-Universität Heidelberg), and then he became a professor of philosophy at the University of Berlin. In 1829, he became the President of the University of Berlin. However, in 1831, at the age of 61, he suddenly passed away after contracting cholera, an infectious disease.

Kant argued that man can only know phenomena and that things can only be perceived as phenomena, but Hegel argued that things themselves can also be known. Hegel believed that all phenomena are beings born of human reason. He also said, "It is meaningful to understand each aspect of the positive and the negative and to go to a higher state and overcome it through its unity," which leads to universal truth. It means the perfect unity between what man perceives and real things in the world, or between subjectivity and objectivity. To put it simply, it means to know the truth. Hegel's concept of the "dialectic" is used for this purpose.

Speaking of Hegel, it is said to be dialectics, and speaking of dialectics, it is said to be Hegel. The origin of dialectics is, of course, Socrates' dialogue, Socratic debate, or Socratic questioning. Dialectic(s) is a gradually developing movement of logic. It proceeds by denying a thesis. According to Hegel, dialectics, our experience itself, gives rise to dialectics. Dialectics is usually expressed in terms of the following diagram: thesis, antithesis, and synthesis. It is a movement of logic that arises from a denial of the initial thesis, but not a total denial. And next, these two sides synthesize or integrate to aim for greater heights for both sides.

Napoleon and Hegel (right)

If you have an idea and you are confronted with an idea that conflicts with your idea, you can progress to a better idea by integrating the two opinions and resolving the contradiction. To put it simply, you can develop your theory by incorporating various values and ideas from a broad perspective without rejecting opinions that differ from yours. To give a commonly used example, suppose you look at an object from above and you perceive its shape as a circle. But suppose it's a rectangle when viewed from the side. Based on these two perspectives, it can be said that the object is a cylinder. Hegel argued that this "dialectics," the mechanism by which theory develops in the wake of conflict,

Hegel

applies not only to dialogue but also to everything in this world. Using the "dialectics," we can overcome the conflict between subjectivity and objectivity and arrive at the truth. Hegel also believed that human history was headed toward the realization of freedom through "dialectics." Every nation always has its own things that are right, morals, ethics, etc. However, if new values are born, contradictions arise. There is no common righteousness, no common values in any era or nation. Therefore, with the passage of the times, we must change what is considered to be correct. In this way, whenever a contradiction arises, humanity repeats the "dialectics" and progresses toward the ideal world.

Diese letzte Gestalt des Geistes, der Geist, der seinem vollständigen und wahren Inhalt zugleich die Form des Selbst gibt und dadurch seinen Begriff ebenso realisiert, wie er in dieser Realisierung in seinem Begriffe bleibt, ist das absolute Wissen; es ist der sich in Geistesgestalt wissende Geist oder das *begreifende Wissen*. Die *Wahrheit* ist nicht nur *an sich* vollkommen der *Gewißheit* gleich, sondern hat auch die *Gestalt* der Gewißheit seiner selbst, oder sie ist in ihrem Dasein, das heißt, für den wissenden Geist in der *Form* des Wissens seiner selbst.[46]

From the standpoint of idealism, Hegel describes in his book, *Phänomenologie des Geistes* (*The Phenomenology of Spirit*) published in 1807,[47] the process of starting from consciousness, recognizing the object itself behind phenomena through dialectics, and becoming the Absolute in which subjectivity and objectivity are integrated. Hegel says that if consciousness changes its knowledge (that is, its relation to the object), so does the object. For new consciousness with transformed knowledge, the object also changes. Because the object belongs to knowledge, the object changes inherently. In this way, our consciousness moves to a higher level. Eventually, objects also change from the way things exist to the law. Consciousness eventually grows into "absolutes Wissen (absolute knowledge)." Consciousness preserves the resolution of contradictions faced in various situations as its results. Thus, the true becomes the whole. Hegel's dialectics of the experience of consciousness has the possibility and path to grow to "Absolute Knowing." Consciousness grows while encountering real objects. And the consciousness that has grown and realized knows that the various objects that we have thought to be opposing are actually ourselves. The reason why we thought that the object was different from us was because there was an aspect of the object that we could not

Hegel in lecture

understand. Consciousness cannot grow by staying with itself, and it can only be realized by making various objects on its own. The path to the true is our self-consciousness, and the true thing that we have acquired at the end of our experience is the entity that spreads out as this world. Consciousness goes beyond the narrow position of personal subjectivity through experience and knows that it is a member of society and part of universality. Through experience, we can grow ourselves into social beings and universal beings. This growth is

Hegel in 1831

also our self-realization. Hegel's philosophy sought to grow the modern individual into an entity that produces higher concepts. This made history meaningful. In other words, truth is the product of the experience of world history.

Das unwesentliche Bewußtsein ist hierin für den Herrn der Gegenstand, welcher die *Wahrheit* der Gewißheit seiner selbst ausmacht. Aber es erhellt, daß dieser Gegenstand seinem Begriff nicht entspricht, sondern daß darin, worin der Herr sich vollbracht hat, ihm vielmehr ganz etwas anderes geworden als ein selbständiges Bewußtsein. Nicht ein solches ist für ihn, sondern vielmehr ein unselbständiges; er also nicht des *Für-sich-Seins*, als der Wahrheit gewiß, sondern seine Wahrheit ist vielmehr das unwesentliche Bewußtsein, und das unwesentliche Tun desselben.[(48)]

In *Part 4, A*, of his *Phänomenologie des Geistes* (IV. Die Wahrheit der

Gewißheit seiner selbst, A. Selbständigkeit und Unselbständigkeit des Selbstbewußtseins, Herrschaft und Knechtschaft), Hegal described the relationship between master (domination) and slave (servitude) and affirmed that the two are in an inverted relationship. Hegal said that the freedom of the master was a façade (seeming) and that in fact the master could not live on his own but depended on the slaves to live. On the contrary, slaves who have skills are not dependent on others. The master and the slave should recognize their need for each other and cooperate with each other. This idea had a significant influence on the later German philosopher Karl Marx (born in 1818) and contributed to the emergence of socialism, which was supported by a large number of people around the world. However, the shortcomings of socialism were gradually discovered, and at the same time, Hegel's "dialectics" and "totalitarianism" that oppresses the individual were criticized. Then an entirely new philosophy began. There are two philosophers who pioneered this process. The German philosopher, Arthur Schopenhauer, born in 1788, rejected Hegel's

"dialectic" by saying that the basis of everything is "Blind Will to Survive." He said, "In this world, all living things,

The birthplace of Hegel in Stuttgart, capital of the Duchy of Württemberg

including humans, are just struggling to live without any meaning, and there is no progress or development there." The Danish philosopher S. A. Kierkegaard, born in 1813, argued that it was better to choose "this or that" rather than dialectical thinking to incorporate "this and that." Kierkegaard wanted to pursue his own truth rather than universal truth.

Hegel was one of the most important figures in German idealism, and European history reached a turning point with Hegel's death. In France, a year before his death, the July Revolution broke out, and a liberal movement developed in Germany after that. The German civil revolution, called the March Revolution, broke out in 1848.

Karl von Hegel (1813-1901) was one of Hegel's three sons. He earned a Ph.D. at the University of Berlin. His doctor's thesis was about Alexander the Great, and he became a well-known historian of the $19^{th}$ century in Germany. Karl also became vice-rector at the University of Erlangen-Nuremberg in 1870.

Hegel's tombstone in Berlin

# 23. A Brief History of Denmark

If you're a fan of English literature, the first thing that comes to mind when you think of Denmark is playwright William Shakespeare's masterpiece "The Tragedy of Hamlet, Prince of Denmark." The fact that the protagonist of Shakespeare's masterpiece is not an English prince but a Danish prince shows that both England and Denmark are deeply connected to each other, ethnically and historically. It is also possible that present-day Denmark and the surrounding areas are the birthplace of Germanic peoples.

"Denmark" means "country of the Danes" (and "Dane" means "low-land"). It is a Nordic country consisting of a small peninsula between the North Sea and the Baltic Sea and the surrounding islands, with a population of six million. Officially, it is the Kingdom of Denmark, which includes the Faroe Islands in the North Atlantic and Greenland in North America. The capital, Copenhagen, is located on the island of Sjælland. In 1167, the fortified city was built by a bishop, marking the beginning of the city's construction. Why did they place the capital on the island? This may be due to the fact that Denmark is a maritime country and that militarily, the island is considered a natural fortress surrounded by

Idun, in North mythology, the keeper of the magic apples of immortality

the sea. In the 1850s, the walls surrounding the city were destroyed.

From around 1,500 BC, Germanic peoples began to live. Later, they became Jutes (north) and Angles (south). Around 500 BC, the Celts brought iron tools. When the

Invitation of the Varangians (Vikings)

Roman Empire was established, furs and amber were exported, and tableware and wine were imported. In the $5^{th}$ century, during the Great Migration of Germanic peoples, the Normans (Northern Germanics) arrived, oppressed, and mixed with the inhabited Angles, Saxons, and Jutes (Western Germanics). They began to be called "Danes." Then they attacked Britain, France, and others with their superior shipbuilding and navigation techniques. From the $8^{th}$ to the $11^{th}$ centuries, the Danes (Danish in modern days) were called Vikings, and they were very feared by their neighboring countries.

In the $11^{th}$ century, King Canute established the North Sea Empire, which included England and Norway. In 1397, the "Kalmar League" united the three kingdoms of Denmark, Norway, and Sweden, with Denmark as its leader. Sweden became independent in 1523, and thereafter it became a bilateral alliance of Denmark and Norway. From the $17^{th}$ to the $20^{th}$ centuries, Denmark had land areas such as Greenland and Iceland, as well as many small islands. It is said that the Denmark East India Company was importing more tea than the British East India Company at that time. However, Denmark began to decline

Viking ship

in 1626 when Denmark intervened in Germany's "Thirty Years' War" and was defeated. In 1814, Denmark lost Norway to Sweden because Denmark allied with France in the Napoleonic Wars (Sweden and Norway became a union of the same monarchy, 1814-1905). In the 19th century, Denmark experienced a golden age of culture, flourishing in the fields of literature, painting, sculpture, and philosophy. It was against this background that the fairy tale writer Hans Christian Andersen (1805-75) and the philosopher Søren Aabye Kierkegaard (1813-55) appeared.

In World War II, the country fought almost no battles and was occupied by Germany (said to be a model-occupied country). Hitler also allowed the Denmark government to continue. Today, Denmark is a small country geographically, but it leads the world as an agricultural and welfare state, and its citizens have the highest

The National Constitutional Assembly was held in 1848 at Christiansborg Palace.

level of life satisfaction in the world. It is also said to be the most digitized country. It is now a stable, developed country as an original member of the North Atlantic Treaty Organization (NATO) and as a member of the European Union (EU). It is also known

Frederiksborg Castle in 1652

in Japan for its educational toys, Lego, and porcelain (china) of Royal Copenhagen. North Sea oil fields and natural gas account for 10% of exports. Other exports include transportation machinery parts, chemical products, and food and livestock (pork bacon). Greenland has abundant metal deposits. 75% of the population belongs to the Church of Denmark. The most popular sport is football. It is also a safe country, ranking fourth in the world after Japan. In the capital city, Copenhagen, many people use bicycles considering environmental

Christiansborg Palace

issues, so it is said to be "the world's number one bicycle city."

The Little Mermaid

H. C. Andersen

Denmark leads the world as a welfare state, with free medical expenses, free maternity expenses and free education (although half of income is taxed). Women's rights are also guaranteed, with 75 to 80 percent of women working (between 16 and 65 years old). In terms of LGBT equality, homosexuality was legalized in 1933. In the late 1980s, same-sex marriage became possible. In 2010, same-sex couples were given the right to adopt. In 2017, it became the first in the world to abolish the treatment of gender identity disorder as a disease. It is not surprising that the Kingdom of Denmark has been rated as the happiest nation on Earth many times in the world happiness rankings.

St. Canute's Cathedral in Odense, where Andersen was born.

# 24. Kierkegaard: An existentialist Hamlet who appeared in the 19<sup>th</sup> century

Søren A. Kierkegaard

The founder of existentialism, Søren Aabye Kierkegaard (1813-55), was a Danish philosopher. His family name 'Kierkegaard' is an earlier spelling of the Danish that means 'Churchyard' or 'Graveyard.' Naturally, unconsciously, the word 'church' had a profound influence on his way of thinking from an early age, and perhaps, because of this, his philosophical views and his real life became inseparable from religion and closely associated with the Christian spirit. He criticized the rational-centric Hegel and sought not to extract truth from abstract concepts but from every individual subjective and concrete existence. He declared for the first time that "I should live like this" instead of "human beings should live like this." Leaning into mysteries incomprehensible by reason, Kierkegaard thrust into the mysteries of God, while later Nietzsche and Sartre turned to atheism. Kierkegaard had a great influence on Heidegger and modern Christian thinkers.

Kierkegaard was born in 1813 to a wealthy merchant (hosiery business and wholesaler of imported goods) family in Copenhagen, Denmark, the youngest of seven children. His mother was his father's second wife, former maid to the first, who died childless. Of the seven siblings, up to five died by the age of 34. His mother also died before he was 21. So, Kierkegaard became convinced that he would die at the age of 33 (or 34). That age coincides with the age at which

Jesus Christ was crucified. It is not surprising that Kierkegaard secretly fantasized about the life of Christ, the Son of God. Kierkegaard, partly due to his father's strict educational policies, was a brilliant child, quick-witted, and excelled in school. He listened to music such as Mozart, loved Greek mythology, Biblical stories, and was well versed in Latin.

> At fifteen when I (Kierkegaard) was in grammar school, I wrote with much unction about the proofs of God's existence and the immortality of the soul, about the concept of faith, about the significance of the miracle. For my *examen artium* (Qualification Exams for University Admission) I wrote an essay on the immortality of the soul for which I was awarded *prae ceteris* (best grade); later I won a prize for an essay on this subject.[49]
>
> *Either/Or* translated by Alastair Hannay

He entered the University of Copenhagen at the age of 17, where he studied theology and philosophy. He also studied liberal arts and science as well. At the age of 24, Kierkegaard met and fell in love with a 14-year-old girl named Regine Olsen (1822-1904). They got engaged, but he broke off the engagement four years later (1841). No one knows exactly why, but perhaps he was so prepared to devote his life to philosophy and the pursuit of truth. When Kierkegaard was 25, his father, who had been passionate about education and strict in discipline, died aged 81. For a short time, Kierkegaard got a post as a secondary school teacher but resigned his post of teaching Latin. Kierkegaard remained financially dependent on his rich family for the rest of his life, writing many books, among which are *Either/Or* (*Enten-Eller: Et Livs Fragment*, 1843), *Two Upbuilding Discourses* (*To opbyggelige Taler*, 1843), *Fear and*

*Trembling* (*Frygt og Bæven*, 1843), *Three Upbuilding Discourses* (*Tre opbyggelige Taler*, 1843), *Four Upbuilding Discourses* (*Fire opbyggelige Taler*, 1844), *Stages on Life's Way* (*Stadier på Livets Vej*, 1845), *Concluding Unscientific Postscript to Philosophical Fragments* (*Afsluttende uvidenskabelig Efterskrift til de philosophiske Smuler*, 1846), *Works of Love* (*Kjerlighedens Gjerninger*, 1847), *Sickness unto Death* (*Sygdommen til Døden*, 1849), and *Practice in Christianity* (*Indøvelse i Christendom*, 1850).

'This sickness is not unto death' (John 11.4). But still Lazarus died. Upon the disciples misunderstanding him when he later added: 'Our friend Lazarus sleepeth, but I go, that I may awake him out of sleep' (11.11), Christ told them bluntly: 'Lazarus is dead' (11.14). So Lazarus is dead, and yet this sickness was not unto death; he was dead, and still this sickness is not unto death. We know, of course, that Christ was thinking of the miracle which, 'if [they] wouldest believe', was to let contemporaries see 'the glory of God' (11.40), that miracle through which he awoke Lazarus from the dead; so 'this sickness' was not merely 'not unto death', but as Christ had foretold, 'for the glory of God, that the son of God might be glorified thereby (11.4). Ah! But even had Christ not awoken Lazarus, is it not still true that this sickness, death itself, is not unto death? When Christ steps forward to the grave and in a loud voice cries out, 'Lazarus, come forth' (11.43), it is plan enough that this sickness is not unto death.[50]

*The Sickness unto Death* translated by Alastair Hannay

Kierkegaard did not object to man as an abstract concept but to man as a concrete factual being. In anxiety, anguish, and despair, he pursued the subjective truth of the individual, that is, the truth only for himself. He said, "The sickness that leads to death is despair," and he believed that no matter what possibilities and ideals we pursued in the real world, we could not avoid the despair brought about by death and that only the possibility of salvation by God could be possible (opposed to the conventional belief that if we believe, we will be saved). Despair is a characteristic that only human beings have, and it is important not to look away from it but to live independently and subjectively. Contrary to Hegel's attempt to capture the world and history as a whole, Kierkegaard argued that each human being has its own essence. He argued that being in history and choosing one's own destiny would not be solved by the abstract theory that Hegel emphasized. Kierkegaard argued that each is determined by everyone's concrete thinking.

> Believe a girl, you will regret it; if you do not believe her, you will also regret it; if you believe a girl or you do not believe her, you will regret both; whether you believe a girl or you do not believe her, you will regret both.[51]
>
> *Either/Or* translated by Alastair Hannay

In our lives, there are times when we can pursue "this and that," but sometimes we need to choose "this or that." In the end, someone falls into despair. Therefore, beyond the ethical way of being, there is the religious way of being, in which man directly confronts God, experiences God as an individual, and achieves his original way of being. Personal experience determines choice. For Hegel, faith is justice, but for Kierkegaard, at some point, faith becomes irrational. To leave judgment to the objectivity of the masses, he said, is to lose oneself. Only God's miracle is believed. In order to overcome the despair that there is no meaning in this world, Kierkegaard once again bet on the miracle of God, the possibility that God exists.

The Glyptotek, a museum in Copenhagen

Though he was a devout Christian, Kierkegaard hated the Danish Church, which placed too much emphasis on formality. Kierkegaard always wanted to live an unconventional life. He believed that going to church every week and praying every night was not the only way to be a devout Christian. In October 1855, during the struggle for reform of the Danish Church, the small and thin Kierkegaard collapsed on the streets of Copenhagen and died in a hospital the following month. He was 42 years old at that time.

During his lifetime, Kierkegaard published a vast number of books. The number of books he published is clearly larger than the number of books published by the great philosophers of the past. However, during his lifetime, he was not popular and ended his life in obscurity. Later, Kierkegaard became a world-famous philosopher because Nietzsche, Sartre and other philosophers in the 20<sup>th</sup> century appreciated Kierkegaard's existentialist ideas. The fact that he was able to publish many books during his lifetime suggests that most of his books were probably self-published.

# 25. History of Germany, Part II

In 1862, Bismarck (Otto von Bismarck, 1815-98), from a Junker landowner (landed nobility), was appointed Chancellor of the Kingdom of Prussia, and in 1871, he established the federal state "German Empire" with the exception of the Austrian Empire by his diplomatic skills. During the unification of Germany, he fought a war with Denmark and won in 1864. He went to war with France, won the war, and took a large amount of compensation in 1870. The following year (1871), Bismarck became the first Imperial Chancellor of the German Empire. Bismarck promoted the production of iron, with which he manufactured cannons and strengthened his army. He suppressed Catholicism and suppressed socialists, but he was in pro-Semitism. He tried to bring education under the control of the state. In diplomacy, he had complex and skillful alliances, and he was always wary of relations between France and Britain. He eventually made France isolated. At the Berlin Conference (1884-85), which was held at the

Bismarch 1

suggestion of Bismarck, the principles of the partition and colonization of Africa by 14 Western nations were discussed, and Bismarck mediated fairly between the powerful nations. In 1890, Bismarck came into conflict with the emperor (Wilhelm II) and was ousted from office (as a result, Germany became internationally isolated). After that, Germany's industry continued to develop, and German products dominated the British market. Eventually, Germany would come into conflict with Russia and France.

In June 1914, the heir to the throne of the Austrian Empire was assassinated in Sarajevo, the capital of Bosnia, and in July, Austria declared war on Serbia. Then Germany, which was an ally of Austria, also entered the war, resulting in a war between two coalitions, the Allies and the Central Powers. The Allies was led by France, the United Kingdom, Russia, the United States, Italy, Japan, and other countries, and the Central Powers were led by the German Empire, Austria-Hungary, the Ottoman Empire, Bulgaria, and other countries.

Bismarch 2

Germany's defeat in the First World War (1914-18) resulted in 10 million German casualties (20 million soldiers and civilians in Europe as a whole). Incidentally, between 50 million and 80 million people were killed in the Second World War. After the Great War (World War I), leftist strikes were frequent. Then, the German Revolution began, and Emperor Wilhelm II abdicated and went into exile. In February 1919, the National Assembly was held in Weimar, a city in Thuringia, a state of central Germany. In June 1919, the Treaty of Versailles was signed with the Allies ceded part of German territory to France, abandoned all German overseas colonies, and reduced large-scale German troops. In addition, a huge reparation payment

Birthplace in Schönhausen

Brandenburger Tor (1871)

(132 billion marks) was added to the treaty. The humiliating terms of the treaty aroused the widespread resentment among the Germans, which later became the cause of World War II.

In August 1919, the Weimar Constitution was enacted, and the Weimar Republic was established, making it the most democratic country in the world. However, after that, inflation did not stop in Germany, and the economy deteriorated significantly. Meanwhile, France demanded reparations from Germany. In 1929, the stock market crashed on Wall Street in New York, leading to the Great Depression. In Germany, the unemployment rate exceeded 30 percent. In 1932, the Nazis became the largest party in the general election, and Adolf Hitler (1889-1945) became Chancellor of Germany. In 1934, Hitler became the sole Führer (Leader) who was both President and Chancellor by national

referendum. Hitler established a one-party dictatorship under the Nazi Party. Hitler abolished the military limitation, introduced conscription, and promoted the expansion of armaments. Eventually, Austria

The proclamation of Wilhelm I as German emperor (1885)

190

was annexed (1938), and the following year, Nazi Germany marched into the Czechoslovakia Republic, established a puppet government in Slovakia, and annexed Czech.

Bezirk Mitte, Berlin

In the same year, Hitler invaded Poland, resulting in the outbreak of World War II (1939). The following year (1940), German troops occupied Denmark and Norway, and then the fall of Paris followed. The German-Soviet War broke out (June 1941), the Declaration of War on the United States was issued (December 11, 1941), and Allied troops landed in Normandy (Normandy Campaign, June 6, 1944). Hitler committed suicide (1945), and in the same year, Germany surrendered unconditionally. By the end of the war, Hitler had killed nearly 6 million Jews in Europe. He also killed 70,000 mentally ill Germans, 500,000 Gypsies, 600,000 Polish soldiers, 3 million Polish civilians, 13 million Russian soldiers (who died on the battlefield), 3 million Russian prisoners of war, and 6 million Russian civilians (including those who starved to death). It is also worth noting that 5 million German soldiers were killed in battle, and 500,000 German civilians died.

After the fall of Nazi Germany, the Allies divided the country into four occupation zones and then divided it into East and West Germany in 1949. East Germany became the German Democratic Republic under political and military control by the Soviet Union, while West Germany became the Federal Republic of Germany, supported by France, the United Kingdom, and the United States. In 1955, during the era of East and West Germany, the Federal Republic of

Angela Merkel (2007)

Germany (West Germany) joined NATO (a military alliance organization), and the Berlin Wall was built in 1961. After the Cold War, they experienced the fall of the Berlin Wall (1989) and the unification of East and West Germany (1990). In 1993, the European Union (EU) was established, and Germany became a member of the EU. In 2005, Angela Merkel (1954-) became Germany's first female chancellor and ruled for 16 years until 2021. Today, Germany has joined hands with its nemesis, France, with whom it has been at war for many years. Both countries reign supreme as the leaders of Europe.

Currently, the Federal Republic of Germany (Bundesrepublik Deutschland) consists of 16 states, with Berlin as its capital, and the population is 83 million (the largest in the EU). Now, Germany has the image of an industrial country and ranks as the third in the world in terms of GDP (2024). Germany

Scenery along the Spree River in Berlin

excelled in science and technology, and Germany invented gasoline cars and diesel engines. Brands such as Mercedes-Benz, Porsche, BMW, Audi, and Volkswagen are famous and have a high reputation worldwide.

In the northern part of Germany, the standard language is spoken, while in the south, the dialect is said to be slightly stronger. In the south, there are fewer large people than in the north, and there are many women who are around 150 cm tall. Their hair

Typical German food

color is brown, and the German national costume that we generally imagine is also that of the south. Speaking of German cuisine, there are sausages, ham, bread, cheese, salted meat, salted cabbage, and beer (drinkable, over 16 years old). Potatoes have been the national food since the 19$^{th}$ century. In the south, wine grapes are produced, and the majority of wines are white, and lots of sweet white wines. In fact, southern Germany has a richer food culture than northern Germany, while in the north, there is a local cuisine made with saltwater fish. The largest religion in Germany is Christianity, accounting for 51% of the population. Of these, 25% are Catholic, 23% are Protestant, and 3% are other Christians. Additionally, 44% of the population has no religious affiliation.

The oldest university in Germany is the University of Heidelberg, founded in 1386. Incidentally, the University of Oxford was founded at the end of the 11$^{th}$ century, and the University of Paris was founded in the 12$^{th}$ century. The University of Munich was founded in 1472, and the University of Berlin was founded in 1810 with the aim of freedom of research and education. Almost all of the universities are state universities (national universities), and there is basically no tuition fee. As for sports, in Germany, football is the most popular one.

# 26. Karl Marx: Materialism

Karl Marx

Charles Robert Darwin (1809-82) studied medicine at the University of Edinburgh and Christian theology at the University of Cambridge's Christ's College. He later became a naturalist, geologist, and then biologist. In 1859, he published *On the Origin of Species*. It was revealed that all species evolved from a common ancestor over a long period of time and that living organisms constantly change to adapt to the environment, compete for survival, and give birth to diverse species (survival of the fittest). If there is no fatal contradiction in explaining the mechanism of the world by assuming that matter is the source of all things, then there is no need to discuss the existence of God. Later, "materialism" began to be supported by many scholars because of the development of the natural sciences. In particular, Darwin's theory of biological evolution influenced many thinkers and philosophers. All living things, including humans, have survived and evolved by species that adapt to their environment through natural selection. According to Darwin's theory, man was not created by God from earth, and man was not special compared to other living beings. Darwin's discovery shocked the world. The beginning of philosophy was to find the root of all things, but mankind has finally revealed that it is matter. It is impossible to completely deny the existence of God, but at least everything in the world can be explained in terms of matter. Humanity has finally figured out where they came from. Philosophers will then challenge themselves to answer the question of where humanity is headed.

### Das Kapital

Karl Marx was born in 1818 in Trier, a territory of the Kingdom of Prussia. His father came from a family of generational Jewish priests, but he was a liberal and converted to Protestantism, making a living as a lawyer. Marx's mother was Dutch-Jewish, and the Marx family was wealthy. He studied law, philosophy, literature, and history at the Universities of Bonn and Berlin. In 1841, he received his doctorate in philosophy. Because he could not become a university professor, he became the editor-in-chief of a newspaper company, which eventually fell out of print. But Marx, who had married the daughter of a Prussian nobleman four years older than him, moved to Paris with his wife and became involved in the running of the magazine's first issue. However, it was discontinued in the first issue, and although he subsequently contributed numerous articles to the journal, Marx was expelled from the country due to his critical views of the government and moved to Brussels, in Belgium. In 1849, he fled to England and studied economics at the British Museum in London. He died in London in 1883, at the age of 64.

Charles Darwin

Marx regarded capital as a common asset of society and the workers who multiplied that capital as agents of social change. The Prussian government was wary of Marx because he was a dangerous revolutionary thinker who aimed for a society of equality without a gap between the rich and the poor, eliminating the distinction between capitalists (the bourgeoisie) who exploited surplus value and workers (the proletariat) who were exploited. Traditionally, it was thought that spiritual forces moved history, but Marx argued that material forces and the development of productive capabilities drive history. This way of thinking is called "historical materialism." He also believed that capitalist society would eventually come to an end and that the era of socialism and communism would come in the future.

Marx was a philosopher of "materialism," who held that everything in this world was governed by matter and that there was no such thing as God, the soul, the afterlife, or Ideas. In other words, it is the idea that there is only matter in the world. Since the cause for everything in this world lies in matter, "justice" and "emotion" in the human mind are also determined by matter. For example, eating delicious food makes the human mind happy because of the substance of delicious food. If you get angry when you are beaten, it is the substance of the fist that creates anger in your heart. Also, suppose that people in a certain country live by catching fish from the sea, and the idea that "you should not catch too much fish" is correct there. That correctness is not a universal truth that is available anywhere in this universe. There is a reason for the substance: if you catch too many fish and destroy the marine ecosystem, it will lead you to food scarcity.

And, of course, Marx argued that the morality of "do not tell a lie," the ethics of "human life must be valued the most," the religious belief that "if you believe in God, you will be saved," and the virtue of "do not seek revenge even if you are wronged or damaged," are all things that matter prescribes. Moreover, the ruling class of the nation can manipulate matters at will, using money and power. To be able to manipulate matter as they wish means to be able to determine the morals, ethics, religious teachings, and justice of a country in their own favor. For example, what about the teachings of religion? "The rich go to hell because they are wicked, and the poor go to heaven because they are good. Under heaven all men are equal." If it is true that you can make it easier in the other world because of the hardship in this world, you will be able to keep the balance. But from the perspective of "materialism," there is no such thing as the other world. Isn't the point that it is a convenient teaching for the ruling class to force the poor to work hard for low wages by saying that they can make it easier in a non-existent heaven because they work and struggle pretty hard in this world?

According to Marx's argument, it can be interpreted as follows: There is no God. That is why we create equality not with God but with the power of man. Then, how can we create equality? Marx cited Hegel's "dialectic" and arranged it. The relationship between management and labor is contradicted by the productive forces that improve with the development of the economy. In other words, even though the company's profits are rising, workers' wages remain the same. Therefore, the disgruntled workers cause a struggle against the ruling class, and working conditions will be improved. Thus, humanity advances through the class

St. Marien-Kirche, Lübeck

struggle that arises whenever contradictions arise. Therefore, Marx insisted that if the workers of the whole world should unite to start a revolution, we would be able to create an ideal socialist country in which all people were equal to each other.

However, we learned that when it came to socialism, the motivation to work declined, and the economy of one socialist country stagnated. In addition, shortcomings such as the danger of becoming a one-party state, a dictatorship, or not being able to freely make political statements were pointed out. In modern times, in liberal countries, many people recognize Marxism as a dangerous idea. However, isn't it premature to underestimate Marx with this? Because when Hegel said that humanity has progressed in "dialectics," he is quite right. Modern capitalism is very different from pre-Marx capitalism. We will not force people to work hard for low wages, and the gap between the rich and the poor is not as severe as it was before. Capitalism, which advocates liberty, has united the good points of the two sides and resolved the contradictions in the face of the opposing idea of socialism. Such an idea advocates equality. Therefore, in modern society, there is capitalism that combines freedom and equality. Maybe Marx had anticipated this. If every time a contradiction arises, it is resolved and mankind progresses. Then, of course, there must be a contradiction in the socialism that he insisted on. And there will be contradictions in modern capitalism at some point. In what Hegel says, there will be no contradictions in an ideal world that realizes true freedom. But it is a story of an endless future. Marx's assertion that a socialist country is an ideal country may have been some tactics to inspire the workers to start a revolution.

*Manifest der Kommunistischen Partei* (*The Communist Manifesto*, 1848), *Das Kapital. Kritik der politischen Ökonomie* (*Capital: Critique of Political*

*Economy,* 1867): These books are Marx's representative works.

## Capitalism and Socialism

The Industrial Revolution that took place in England at the end of the 18th century opened up a new era and brought enormous benefits to mankind. On the other hand, the poor were forced to work long hours by capitalists who were only interested in making money. The environment was so harsh and cruel that the average life expectancy of the working class in Britain sometimes fell below 20 years in the 19th century. Has the development of science really made people happy? What lies beyond human progress? At a time when everyone began to question what they had believed to be right and the raison d'être (the purpose of life) of themselves and society, Marx emerged.

Marx came to the conclusion that a socialist state was the ideal, and he incited the workers to revolution. Eventually, many people all over the world sympathized with Marx's ideas. The bourgeois were no exception, and the so-called intellectuals were also followers. However, when the lid was lifted, many socialist states in Europe became dictatorships and were far from ideal countries. What did socialism go wrong with? And why did the intelligentsia at that time support socialism? As it turns out, both capitalism and socialism have their merits and demerits. And it was the capitalist state that succeeded in overcoming those flaws and incorporating the merits of both.

Marx's thought was influenced by Hegel's dialectics, which is the key to solving the problem of the struggle between capitalism and socialism. Dialectics is a way of thinking in which, when a conventional way of thinking (thesis) is confronted with a way of thinking that contradicts it (antithesis), if the two theories are integrated, they will develop into a better way of thinking (synthesis). If we take a bird's-eye view of the history of Europe according to this dialectic, it is as follows: The Industrial Revolution gave birth to one thesis. It was called capitalism, and its idea was to value "freedom" and "free competition." However, as a result, everyone earned money "freely," and a world of the poor and the rich was formed. And the weak in society suffered unimaginably. Therefore, Marx presented the antithesis called socialism, which respects "equality." Capitalism, which makes people work like disposable tools, has no future. If that is the case, then we should become socialist, which is not "free" but "equal." However, if you only assert your own opinion and do not listen to the opinions of others, you will not make progress. Dialectics is the development of one's own theory by incorporating ideas that are different from one's own. Capitalist countries accepted "equality" without turning away from the antithesis called socialism. The British Labour Party raised the slogan "from cradle to grave," and welfare and labor standards laws were born. In this way, a new form of capitalism was completed that balanced "freedom" and "equality." Of course, this is not to say that British society today is perfect and does not need to change any more. There is still a lot of work to be done, and we should continue to work on the next step dialectically.

British Museum

# 27. **Nietzsche:** Gott starb (God died)

Friedrich Nietzsche

Friedrich Wilhelm Nietzsche was born in 1844 in the Prussian Plovinz Sachsen to a wealthy Lutheran pastor. When Nietzsche was five years old, his father died. He studied theology, philosophy, and classical philology at the University of Bonn but stopped believing in God along the way, so he abandoned his theological studies. While at university, he transferred to the University of Leipzig (Universität Leipzig). In 1864, at the age of 24, he became a professor at the University of Basel (Universität Basel), teaching classical philology on ancient Greece. However, after working at the university for 10 years, he resigned his job due to ill health and other factors. From then on, he entered a life of writing.

Nietzsche was an atheistic existentialist. The Danish philosopher Kierkegaard (1813-55) is said to be the father of existential philosophy, but he was a theistic existentialist. For Kierkegaard, despair was a "deadly disease" in which he saw the possibility of living in faith. Nietzsche said that, unlike Kierkegaard, God or Christian values are no longer useful in modern society. Nietzsche's position was nihilism that completely denied European philosophy. The faith of surrendering everything to God is the same as that of a slave. Morality is the value that the weak unilaterally label the strong as the bad guys and gain mental superiority. Christianity is a missionary based on the weak, that the punishment falls on the strong, and that if their daily deeds are good, the weak can go to heaven. Nietzsche denied life after death, and he thought that this world is meaningless and repeats itself endlessly. However, he said that the important thing is not to rely on God's existence there, but to think for yourself and live by your own power. Nietzsche was really a pioneer of "existentialism." Speaking of Nietzsche, we easily feel the image of a pessimistic philosopher who coined the quote "God died," but that is a big mistake. His quote continues.

Gott starb: nun wollen *wir*-daß der Übermensch lebe.[52]

(God died: now *we* want the superhuman to live.)

In the same book, Also sprach Zarathustra (Also spoke Zarathustra), Nietzsche explains "God" and "superhuman" as follows:

Einst sagte man Gott, wenn man ich auf ferne Meere blicket; nun aber lehrte ich euch sagen: Übermensch. Gott ist eine Mutmaßung; aber ich will, daß euer Mutmaßen nicht weiter reiche, als euer scaffender Wille. Könntet ihr einen Gott schaffen? — So schweigt mir doch von allen Göttern! Wohl aber könntet ihr den Übermenschen schaffen.[53]

Here, Nietzsche said that "God" was only a speculation, that we should no longer talk about "God," and that we should use the word "superman" instead of "God." Instead of creating a single "God," we should create many "superhumans."

I would like to explain in order what the death of God is and what the superhuman is. In modern times, with the development of natural science, the existence of God became shabby, and the influence of Christianity also weakened. In order to convince modern people that there is no God, Nietzsche described this situation as "God died." He argued that the idea of Christianity came from the "Ressentiment" of the weak. "Ressentiment" means jealousy, bitterness, or resentment. In other words, the poor and others were jealous of the rich and powerful, and by believing in Christianity that used beautiful words such as "equality" and

Nietzsche (1861)

"philanthropy," they justified themselves, the weak, and blamed the strong who had money. The weak regarded the strong as evil. Besides Christianity, Nietzsche rejected all the values and traditions that emerged from "Ressentiment." And then comes the idea of nihilism that if there

is no God, there is no meaning to man's birth, and that there is no value in living. But the gist of Nietzsche's thought is not the nihilism of "God died" but the overcoming of nihilism: "Then what should we do now?" You will see that he is not pessimistic but a philosopher with a very positive personality. Then, in a world without God, what should we humans live for?

Nietzsche argued that human beings should accept the fate that they have no choice but to live in this meaningless and

Nietzsche (1868)

Left to right: Lou Salomé, Paul Rée and Nietzsche (1882)

aimless world and that they should become ideal persons, or Übermenschen (superhumans), who can create their own meaning and purpose for living. The philosophies that began with Socrates were studies of searching for answers to God's problems, such as "What kind of way of life is right?," "What is the structure of this world?," or "Why were people born?" But philosophy after Nietzsche changed to the discipline of "there is no answer because there is no God, man creates the answer." Such ideas are called "existentialism." In 1900, Nietzsche contracted pneumonia and died at the age of 55.

# 28. Heidegger: We Should Live in a Finite Time as Ourselves

Martin Heidegger

Martin Heidegger was a German philosopher who was born in rural Meßkirch, Germany, in 1889. His father was a barrel maker and also worked for the church. Heidegger studied theology at the University of Freiburg but changed his major to philosophy along the way. He published *Sein und Zeit* (*Being and Time*) in 1927 and argued that human beings should face up to the fact that they are beings to death. And also, he pointed out that instead of thinking about nothing and spending time idly but cherishing the limited time, they have to live seriously. The meaning of the world to him as an existentialist was not for the objective world but for the world manifested in the subjectivity of the individual, a world that appeared according to the interests of the individual. He argued that it is important to decide for oneself the path one should take.

Heidegger became rector at the University of Freiburg in 1933 but was expelled from the university for a time after World War II for his support of the Nazi Party. Modern philosophy, which began with Descartes, was dominated by discussions of "epistemology," but Heidegger focused on "ontology," which considers existence. And before delving deeper into what existence is, he said it is essential to analyze the existence of human beings who are interested in existence and thinking about existence, like Kierkegaard and Nietzsche. Some humans tried to understand the meaning of existence and have been facing the question of existence since the days of Greek philosophy. Heidegger named this existence of human being who knows the concept of existence, "Da-sein." "Da-sein" means "there being," "being there," "being-in-the-world," or just "existence." And he preached the right way of life as "Da-sein." Human beings as "Da-sein" feel "anxious" just by living in this world because there is no meaning in this world. Even if you live in a meaningless world, there is no reason to exist. In order to forget this "anxiety," "Da-sein" obscures one's existence by not having one's own opinion, not judging things by one's own will, and so on. Specifically, we believe that what the majority of people decide is right, we think what the masses say is beautiful, and we live in such a way that we imitate what others around us are doing. That way, even if you are replaced by a stranger the next day, your existence will not change much. Heidegger called "Da-sein," who has lost sight of himself in order to alleviate "anxiety," as "Das Man" (the worldly man). Das Man is not aware of his own death, who is busy with his daily life worrying about immediate events. He spends every day on a makeshift basis. In other words, his way of life is like a way of life that is already dead.

Then, how can we find ourselves as different from others? Heidegger realized that death was one's own and could not be exchanged with anyone. In other words, thoughts, actions, experiences, etc. can be imitated by others, but only one's own death is possessed by one's own existence. *Time* finds its meaning in death. Therefore, if you are always conscious that you are a being who is heading toward death, you can live in a finite time as yourself. When you realize that death can come at any moment, you can establish a true self.

Heidegger says in his book, *Being and Time*, that "Da-sein" is a state of

"Sein zum Tode" (being towards an end). He points out that death always comes to everyone. And we never know when we're going to die. Death cannot be exchanged with anyone, and a true self cannot be exchanged with anyone, too. Therefore, death is the most unique possibility for "Da-sein." It is only when we face our own death that we can understand that we are original. To think about the possibility of death is to think about living. Because we don't know anything about life after death, it's impossible to get a complete view of "Da-sein." So, we tend to try to understand the meaning of death by analyzing the deaths of others, but Heidegger denies it. No matter how much we analyze the deaths of others, we cannot find the meaning of our own deaths. It is quite possible to grasp the whole picture of one's existence just by realizing that we are just beings who are going to die. Death is the possibility of our own existence. It is important to aim for some kind of possibility in the form of anticipation. What does death mean to us? It is meaningful in how we live.

All of us, without exception, are part of the world we live in. We can't change that world, but in fact, that world is not objective, and we can change and express the meaning of the world according to our interests. In this context, we should always ask ourselves what we are living for. Accept your past, think about your future potential, and choose actions that match your interests. We are scared of dying, but we can't look away from it. We should always be aware that we are the ones who will inevitably die and those who are going to die, think about how we will live in the present, and live strongly to live our lives for that purpose. We should cherish the limited time we have and live our lives to the fullest. Heidegger died in Meßkirch, West Germany, in May of 1976, at the age of 86.

# 29. History of France, Part II

When the American Revolution (1775-83) began, Louis XVI initially took a wait-and-see approach, but in 1778, he joined the Franco-American alliance to cooperate in the war. As a result, the financial burden on the country increased, and various expenses, such as pensions to support the lives of the court aristocracy, threatened the country's finances. The lives of the peasants were impoverished, and the bourgeoisie also suffered from heavy taxes. In 1789, the Parisians revolted (storming the Bastille), and the French Revolution broke out. After the Declaration of Human Rights, Louis XVI and his queen Marie Antoinette were executed by guillotine. It was called a bourgeois revolution,

but in reality, it was interpreted as a revolution in which the rebellion of the aristocracy against the royal authority, the antipathy of the bourgeois against the aristocracy, the food riots of the urban people, and the land riots of the peasants occurred at the same time. France abolished the monarchy and became a republic.

In 1799, a coup d'état brought Napoleon Bonaparte, a military officer from Corsica, to power in the republic. In 1804, he was crowned

Napoleon Bonaparte

emperor by referendum (Napoleon

summoned Pope Pius VII to Paris, and at the coronation he took the crown from the Pope's hands and placed it on his own head), and he began the Napoleonic Wars. Napoleon was defeated at the Battle of Trafalgar in 1805 but succeeded in the fall of the Prussian royal

*Liberty Leading the People*

capital of Berlin. However, he failed to march into Russia in 1812, and in the end, Napoleon was completely overthrown by the defeat at the Battle of Waterloo.

Louis XVIII of the Bourbon dynasty ascended the throne and a constitutional monarchy appeared. The July Revolution (1830) started the monarchy (the July Monarchy), but the peasants and workers caused the February Revolution (1848), which collapsed the monarchy, and the Second Republic was established. In the midst of the unstable régime, Louis Napoleon became president of the Second Republic, but a coup d'état was staged, and he ascended the throne in 1852 as Napoleon III. The Industrial Revolution progressed, and the economy stabilized, but in the Franco-Prussian War (1870-71), France was defeated, and Napoleon III abdicated. Then, France became the Third Republic (1871-1940). It expanded its colonies to Africa and other countries. Around this time, artists gathered in Paris, and a group of painters called Impressionists, such as Monet, Renoir, and Cézanne, were energetically active in Paris. Delacroix's *Liberty Leading the People* (1830), which depicts the July Revolution, is a masterpiece of Romantic paintings.

General de Gaulle

In World War I, France fought against the German Empire and suffered 1.4 million casualties. In World War II, the country was attacked and defeated by Nazi Germany, and the Third Republic collapsed and came under the control of Germany. After World War II (1946), the right-wing General de Gaulle (Charles de Gaulle), who became the head of the provisional government, formed a coalition cabinet consisting of three parties, including the Communist Party, which contributed the most to the resistance movement during the Nazi rule, but suddenly de Gaulle resigned, and then the Fourth Republic was established by referendum (although the cabinet of "no frills policy" continued for a long time).

In 1959, the Fifth Republic was established, which included strong presidential powers, and Charles de Gaulle became the first president. (De) Gaullism was very close to Bonapartism (Napoleon Bonaparte's political activities). De Gaulle then ruled France for 10 years. An important figure in France's postwar social influence was the Communist Party (known as the "eldest daughter of Moscow"). The Communist Party remained the number one party in elections until the advent of President Mitterrand of the Socialist Party in 1981. This was not only because of its legacy of armed resistance against Nazi Germany but also because intellectuals such as Aragon, Picasso, Curie, and Sartre gave intellectual authority to the communists. In 1960, almost all African colonies became independent. France also gave up its colonies in Indochina during the Vietnam War. After Mitterrand, Jacques René Chirac became president, who inherited de Gaulle's line.

Nowadays, France, officially the French Republic (République française), is racially described as a mixture of the Celts, the Greeks, the Latins (Romans), and the Germans. Unlike the United Kingdom, the Germanic tribes

Eiffel Tower

Arc de triomphe

were a minority, but they were in the ruling class. Even today, discrimination against Asians is said not to disappear. There are many Jewish university professors, lawyers, doctors, merchants, and artists. Seventy percent of the population is Catholic. In order to solve the labor shortage, a large number of immigrants are accepted from former colonies and other countries. With a population of about 68 million and the world's fifth-largest GDP (2020), the capital city of Paris is also a cultural and artistic capital that attracts many tourists every year (the number of tourists entering the country is the first in the world).

The Palace of Versailles (le château de Versailles) was built by Louis XIV, who was called the Sun King. It is said that the court culture in this palace is deeply connected to the present-day manners of French cuisine and meals. Mont Saint-Michel, Notre Dame Cathedral (where many

Cathédrale Notre-Dame de Paris

successive kings were crowned), the Eiffel Tower (the centerpiece of the Paris World's Fair), the Arc de Triomphe de l'Étoile (built by Napoleon in 1806), the Louvre Museum, and the castles in the Loire (les châteaux de la Loire) are popular tourist attractions. In addition, France is a cultural nation that is recognized by everyone as leading the world in fashion, art, and cuisine. As for fashion, fashion brands such as Givenchy, Saint Laurent, Christian Dior, Chanel, Louis Vuitton, and Hermès are very popular worldwide for clothing, shoes, bags, perfumes, accessories, etc., and are always attracting the attention of fashion magazines around the world. As for art, starting with the murals of the "Lascaux Cave" (Grotte de Lascaux), France is a thriving art center, mainly oil paintings, and many artists from all over the world gathered in Paris to engage in creative activities. Claude Lorrain of classicism positioned landscape painting as his specialty and painted "ideal landscapes." The Rococo style of the 18th century abandoned heavy classicism and replaced it with a light and graceful painting world. It depicts a world that is light and graceful (and becomes more pleasurable and erotic). After that, the French Revolution occurred in the 19th century, and classicism was revived again, and it is called Neoclassical style. For example, *Napoleon at the Saint-Bernard Pass* (*Bonaparte franchissant le Grand-Saint-Bernard*) by Jacques-Louis

Louvre Museum

David in 1801. Then, Romanticism appeared, which prioritized color and emphasized the senses, feelings, thoughts, and individuality of the painter. The best example is Delacroix's *Liberty Leading the People* (*La Liberté guidant le peuple*). And in the middle of the 19th century, Realism appeared. Famous works include Courbet's *A Burial of Ornans* (*Un enterrement à Ornans*), which depicted human reality as a new historical painting; Manet's *Olympia*, which depicted the nude body of a prostitute; and Millet's *The Gleaners* (*Des glaneuses*), which depicted the reality of poor farming villages. Impressionism includes Monet's *Impression, Sunrise* (*Impression, soleil levant*) and *Water Lilies* (*Nymphéas*), and Renoir's *Bal du moulin de la Galette* and *Portrait of Iréne Cahen d'Anvers* (*La Petite Iréne*). Post-Impressionism includes Vincent van Gogh's *Sunflowers* and *The Starry Night*, Paul Gauguin's *Still-Life with Fruit and Lemons* and *Delightful Land*, and Paul Cézanne's *Curtain, Jug and Fruit Bowl*. And others are Symbolism, Japonisme, Fauvisme, Art Nouveau, Art Déco, and Surrealism (Surréalisme). The sculptor Auguste Rodin (1840-1917) was also born in France. Rodin is famous for his bronze sculpture, *The Thinker* (*Le Penseur*), and considered the founder of modern sculpture. Of course, the statue of *The Thinker* symbolizes philosophy.

In music, the impressionist composer Claude Debussy (1862-1918) put an end to the history of Western classical music, and from the 1950s, music called chanson became popular. Nowadays, in France, American jazz and British rock are also popular. The film (cinematograph), invented by the Lumière brothers between 1895 and 1905, originated in France and has attracted worldwide

Claude Debussy

Albert Camus

attention, for example, at the Cannes Film Festival (Festival de Cannes). As for literature, in the 19th century, Stendhal's *The Red and the Black* and Victor Hugo's *Les Misérables* appeared, and in the 20th century, Marcel Proust's *In Search of Lost Time*, Antoine de Saint-Exupéry's *The Little Prince* (*Le Petit Prince*), Albert Camus (1913-60)'s *The Stranger* (*L'Étranger*), and Maurice Leblanc's *Arsène Lupin* appeared.

France also leads the world in cuisine, featuring breads such as baguette, bâtard, and croissant, as well as cheeses, wines, brandy, cognac, and café culture. The harvests of fertile land, such as wheat, barley, corn, potatoes, and sugar beets, are plentiful. France is the second-largest exporter of agricultural products in the world.

Sorbonne University (Sorbonne Université) is renowned as a prestigious school. It was originally built in 1257 by Robert de Sorbon (1201-74), chaplain to the court of King Louis IX, for poor clergy to achieve the rank of doctor. In 2018, Paris-Sorbonne University and the University of Pierre et Marie Curie merged to form Sorbonne University. Thirty-three researchers or associates of the university have been awarded the Nobel Prize. The university is ranked 60th in the world (2023).

Popular sports are soccer, rugby, cycling, car racing, skiing, surfing, and judo. 30 percent of couples are legally married, and 40 percent are common-law married. France had many colonies in Asia and Africa, many of which became independent in the 20th century. However, Martinique in Central America,

Guinea in South America, Réunion in the Indian Ocean, Tahiti and New Caledonia in the South Pacific, etc. are still French overseas territories. So, France is one of the world's leading maritime power

La Seine à Paris

nations. It is also a country with a strong military force, officially possessing nuclear weapons, nuclear-powered aircraft carriers, and nuclear submarines.

*Luncheon of the Boating Party* by Renoir

# 30. Sartre: L'existence précède l'essence

Jean-Paul Sartre

Jean-Paul Sartre was born in Paris, France, in 1905. His father, a naval officer, died of an illness when Sartre was two years old. In 1938, he published the novel *La Nausée* (*Nausea*). In 1943, he published *L'Être et le néant: Essai d'ontologie phénoménologique* (*Being and Nothingness: An Essay on Phenomenological Ontology*). And when World War II ended, Sartre's existentialism quickly spread throughout the world, fascinating many young people and creating an existentialist boom. Later, Sartre turned to Marxism and communism. With the rise of structuralism, Sartre's ideas came under criticism.

Sartre said, "L'existence précède l'essence," (Existence precedes essence) in his book recording the lecture and discussion that Sartre gave in Paris in 1945.[54] He said that since God has not given us an essence in advance, we can determine the essence by our own will, so we can build our own essence with our own power and open up our own life. In addition, he insisted that we should change society for the better with our own power. Existentialism is humanism, he said. Sartre, who was credited with establishing existentialist literature, was awarded the Nobel Prize in Literature in 1964 but declined the award.

Existence refers to the existence of humans; essence refers to the character of the person; and this means the purpose of life. Sartre said, "Existence precedes essence," which means that human beings are not necessarily born into this world for some reason and exist without being given any meaning. Many non-human things exist for a reason. For example, chairs were made to sit, pens were made to write, and clocks were made to check the time. But humans were not created by God for a purpose. Therefore, a human is a free being who can choose for himself what he or she lives for, and every human being can become what he or she wants to be because he is nothing at first. This idea is similar to the theory of Nietzsche, a pioneer of existentialism. But the difference between Nietzsche's superhuman thought and Sartre's existentialism is the interpretation of God. Nietzsche tried desperately to deny God, saying that Christianity originated from "ressentiment" of the weak. Certainly, it is undesirable to blindly believe in God and to abandon the idea of thinking about the meaning of our birth.

However, it is true that Christianity has saved many people and that various cultures have been born. It is good to be independent of God, but it would be a thoughtless idea to deny God entirely. In my opinion, human history is similar to the life of a person. Just as children become independent from the parents who raise them, humanity, too, will become independent of God. Nietzsche's time was a period of rebellion in a man's life. This is probably why the radical idea of "God died," that is, to deny one's parents and

Left to right: Simore de Beauvoir, Sartre and Che Guevara

become independent, came about. Sartre, on the other hand, said that existentialism is not atheism in the sense that it tries to prove to the best of its power that God does not exist, but rather it declares that even if God exists, nothing will change, and that is our point of view. We do not believe that God exists, but the problem of God's existence is not the problem.

> L'existentialisme n'est pas tellement un athéisme au sens où il s'épuiserait à démontrer que Dieu n'existe pas. Il déclare plutôt : même si Dieu existait, ca ne changerait rien ; voilà notre point de vue. Non pas que nous croyions que Dieu existe, mais nous pensons que le problème n'est pas celui de son existence ;[55]

It does not matter if there is a God or not. Sartre is trying to convey that the important thing is to form oneself subjectively. He also recommends everyone for *engagement* (social participation) after creating a meaning for life. The theories of Nietzsche and Heidegger give the impression that in order to establish one's true self, one leaves the mundane world and lives in solitude, but Sartre is different. He declared that a person should choose to live in a secular society, influence society, and remake society. Also, in the process of getting involved with society and interacting with others, it will be good for a person to incorporate various opinions. Looking at this mechanism by which people with diverse values gather and influence each other to form a society, we realize that Hegel's "dialectic," rejected by Schopenhauer and Kierkegaard, has been revived in a different form in this period. In fact, Sartre published his *Critique de la Raison Dialectique* (*Critique of Dialectical Reason*) in 1960 and attempted to combine existentialism and Marxism.

However, Sartre's theory of human subjectivity was later criticized by the concept of the *unconscious* advocated by the Austrian psychiatrist Sigmund Freud (1856-1939) and *structuralism* advocated by the French anthropologist Claude Lévy-Strauss (1908-2009). In addition, the French philosopher Jean-François Lyotard (1924-1998) called the philosophies of Hegel and Marx, whose themes had been the structure of the world and ideal countries, "grand narratives." Lyotard rejected the search for such universal truths as leading to totalitarianism, and conflicts and disputes may arise. He argued that in the coming era, "little narratives" that think about the way of life and righteousness of each individual human being are appropriate.

At the age of three, Sartre was almost blind in his right eye, and at the age of 68 (1973), he became blind in his left eye and completely blind in both eyes. He died in 1980, at the age of 74.

## What Sartre wanted to say in *QU'EST-CE QUE LA LITTÉRATURE?*

Sartre published the book *What is Literature?* (*Qu'est-ce que la littérature?*) in 1948. In this

Beauvoir and Sartre

very interesting book, what exactly does the author, Sartre, say the meaning of literature? In short, for Sartre, the ideal literature is one that does not bind the reader. He respected the free will of people above all else and believed that writers should not expect the reader to be delighted or sad in the development of their stories. The interpretation of the work is up to the reader to interpret, and the author should not interfere with it. In *What is Literature?*, Sartre laments that the readers of literary works are only bourgeois. Moreover, to realize a socialist state, he invisions, he is determined to disintegrate the bourgeoisie, just like the favor with a vengeance. Sartre asserts that writers have now become very influential figures in society; literature must reach the masses. Literature, however, is not in the service of the Communist Party. It is difficult to remain a writer and be a communist. There is no guarantee that literature is immortal, but at the same time it can be understood to mean that there is no guarantee that man is not immortal. Literature is fundamentally heretical, and literature makes people reflect and ponder, see their own unstable situation, and constantly try to correct and improve it. Literature, which is the art of writing, is not protected by God's providence. It is something that human beings choose and create for themselves. It should never be propaganda, nor should it be entertainment or distraction. Finally, Sartre concludes the book with the following ironic passage. He would like to say that human beings are very troublesome beings, and literature and human beings are inseparable.

Bien sûr, tout cela n'est pas si important: le monde peut fort bien se passer de la littérature. Mais il peut se passer de l'homme encore mieux. [56]

*Of course, all that is not so important: the world can very well do without literature. But the world can do even better without man.*

Originally, Sartre's perception would have been that a communist society was just better than a capitalist society. Society is constantly changing and progressing. Therefore, literary people, who are always supposed to express themselves from a free standpoint, should not belong anywhere. Just as novelists should not bind their readers, no great political assertion should bind the writer by a single principle. Isn't that what Sartre really meant?

Beautiful cityscape of Paris

# Conclusion

The beginning of ancient Greek philosophy was a question of gods. Until then, they had not thought of an answer to the question because they believed that anything they did not understand in the world was created by gods and was gods' will. However, as the citizens of Athens gained the leisure to contemplate, they began to search for answers to the question on their own. Thus began the history of philosophy, which built up universal truths one step at a time. At first, Thales said, "Everything in the world is made of water." Then Pythagoras appeared. Philosophy later developed into the natural sciences. Then came Christianity, and in medieval Europe, ancient philosophy was sealed, and the center of medieval scholarship became theology. The university originally began as an educational institution attached to a medieval Christian monastery. The University of Paris was founded in the 12th century as a cathedral school, teaching theology and philosophy (and in the 19th century,

RKU Ryugasaki Campus

teaching humanities, law, economics, science, and medicine). European universities subsequently developed on the basis of four faculties: theology, philosophy, letters (literature), and medicine. But at the end of the 20th century, with the exception of some universities, theological and philosophical faculties were absorbed into the Faculty of Literature. Novelists have come to be touted around the world as a glamorous profession, but what supported the popularity of novelists was the echo of the existentialist idea that, in the context of philosophical history, "the meaning of human life is not to seek the answer to it in the Bible, not to seek the words spoken by the pastor of the church, but to think for oneself, by your own strength," and the

Demosthenes

novel was like a report of the practice of that idea. Each novelist wrote about their own experiences, created historical figures and fictional heroes, and interpreted them in various ways to know what it means to live and to tell readers the facts. Writers' works functioned well in society as a whole. Reading novels was an ethical and moral education for those who stopped going to church. Instead of reading the Bible or philosophical books, people read literary works. However, in the 21$^{st}$ century, the Faculty of Literature has lost much of popularity, and the names of the Faculty of Foreign Languages, the Faculty of Humanities, and the Faculty of International Liberal Studies are popular. Novels become mere entertainment, squeezed by comics, anime, and manga. Who will replace the role played by former novelists, in the 21$^{st}$ century?

The philosophy has developed over a long period of history through the repetition of the denial of conventional conclusions. Through Nietzsche, Sartre, a structuralist Lévy-Strauss, and the standard-bearer of postmodernism, Lyotard, the mainstream of philosophy has led to a conservative view that overly prioritizes the individual rather than grasping society as a whole. Structuralism dwarfed individuals by claiming that human beings are dominated by something invisible and unconscious, that is, by some hidden structure, the surrounding environment, and the social structure, and that individuals can never decide anything freely by their own will. However, it is inconceivable that this point of arrival will be forever correct. Once again, there will be progressive philosophers who will argue "grand narratives." Hegel and Marx said that humanity progresses whenever contradictions arise in history. In other words, when there is no contradiction, there is no change, and human history is a repetition of maintaining the status quo and breaking it. So, the time of the progressive philosophers, Marx and Sartre, did not last forever. Nevertheless, to put it another way, if the era without change continues, it means that the time will come to change society again. However, Marx had the radical idea that social change would occur through class struggle. In the novel *Crime and Punishment* by the Russian novelist Dostoevsky (1821-81), a contemporary of Marx, the protagonist Raskolnikov murders a Jewish old usurer with the idea that a chosen one with the talent to rule the country in the future can

commit crime. Both were dangerous ideas that were willing to sacrifice for the sake of human progress. Unfortunately, looking back on history, it is true that many great men who have made great contributions to humanity and so-called heroes have taken the lives of many people. However, this may have been unavoidable in the days of Marx and Dostoevsky, and in today's world, where freedom of expression is guaranteed, at least in a liberal state, it is possible to peacefully reshape

Rodin's "The Thinker"

society. In fact, Sartre was a reformer, but he did not commit crimes and did not incite violent revolution. I think that the philosophy of the future will be a mixture of "little narratives" and "grand narratives," in which people think about the meaning of their lives with their own power and put them into practice, albeit in a small way. At the same time, each person participates in society and eventually makes a grand narrative. It is important to pursue both, not just one. And we will create our own great stories for the future.

Today, we often hear the word "diversity." I think it is a trend to acknowledge values that cannot be understood, but it is a mistake to admit anything unnecessarily. Isn't that where chaos and disorder are going? After all, at first, it may seem like something completely different, but there is actually a common universal value at the root of it. We don't just need to acknowledge different worlds, but we need to constantly seek out common concepts and people who resonate with each other, and the world will be a little better.

# NOTES

(1) J. E. Morpurgo ed., *Keats: Poems* (Penguin Books, 1953), p.193.

(2) *Ibid.*, p.210.

(3) *Ibid.*, p.212.

(4) Charles James Stuart, *The Holy Bible: Authorized King James Version* (Oxford University Press, 1993), p.9.

(5) *Ibid.*, p.970.

(6) *The Holy Bible: English Standard Version* (Crossway, 2001), p.330.

(7) *Ibid.*, p.379.

(8) *Ibid.*, p.454.

(9) *Ibid.*, p.464.

(10) Charles James Stuart, *The Holy Bible: Authorized King James Version* (Oxford University Press, 1993), p.974.

(11) *Ibid.*, p.1170.

(12) *Ibid.*, p.1173.

(13) *Ibid.*, p.1246.

(14) *The Holy Bible: English Standard Version* (Crossway, 2001), p.595.

(15) Charles James Stuart, *The Holy Bible: Authorized King James Version* (Oxford University Press, 1993), p.1264.

(16) Francis Bacon, *Complete Essays of Francis Bacon* (Independently published, 2017), p.175.

(17) John Locke, *An Essay Concerning Humane Understanding* (Independently published, 2019), pp.lxviii-lxix.

(18) David Hume, *David Hume Collection: A Treatise of Human Nature, An Enquiry Concerning Human Understanding, and Dialogues Concerning Natural Religion* (Independently published/Amazon.co.jp, 2020), p.111.

(19) *Ibid.*, p.4.

(20) *Ibid.*, p.42.

(21) J. G. Lockhart, *Memoirs of the Life of Sir Walter Scott, Bart 7 vols.* (Vol.1 〜 Vol.4: Boston: Otis, Broaders, and company, 1837. / Vol.5 〜 Vol.7: Philadelphia: Carey, Lea & Blanchard, 1838), *Vol.2*, p.166.

(22) Walter Scott, *Waverley* (Penguin Books, 1994), p.400.

(23) *Memoirs of the Life of Sir Walter Scott, Bart 7 vols, Vol.1*, p.28.

(24) James Logie Robertson ed., *The Poetical Works of Sir Walter Scott* (Oxford University Press, 1916) p.250.

(25) Fiona Robertson ed., *Lives of the Great Romantics II, Keats, Coleridge & Scott by Their Contemporaries* (Pickering & Chatto, 1997) *Vol.3 Scott*, pp.148-50.

(26) *Memoirs of the Life of Sir Walter Scott, Bart 7 vols, Vol.5*, p.49.

(27) "Few names deserve more honourable mention in the history of Scotland during this period, than that of John, Duke of Argyle and Greenwich." From Walter Scott, *The Heart of Mid-Lothian* (Penguin Books, 1994), p.360.

(28) ⋯but he [Jeffrey] wants [is short of] that enthusiastic feeling which like sunshine upon a landscape lights up every beauty, and palliates, if it cannot hide, every defect. From *Familiar Letters of Sir Walter Scott 2 vols* (David Douglas, 1894) *Vol.1*, p.128.

(29) Fiona Robertson ed., *Lives of the Great Romantics II, Keats, Coleridge & Scott by Their Contemporaries* (Pickering & Chatto, 1997) *Vol.3 Scott*, p.160.

(30) *Memoirs of the Life of Sir Walter Scott, Bart 7 vols, Vol.4*, p.202.

(31) *Ibid., Vol.3*, p.104.

(32) *Ibid., Vol.4*, p.128.

(33) *Ibid., Vol.6*, p.213.

(34) *Ibid., Vol.3*, pp.103-104.

(35) *The Poetical Works of Sir Walter Scott* (Oxford University Press, 1916), p.37.

(36) *Memoirs of the Life of Sir Walter Scott, Bart 7 vols, Vol.6*, p.129.

(37) J. G. Lockhart abridged and newly edited, *The Life of Sir Walter Scott* (Hutchinson & Co., 1848), p.201.

(38) *Memoirs of the Life of Sir Walter Scott, Bart 7 vols, Vol.6*, p.126.

(39) David Daiches, *Sir Walter Scott and His World* (Thames & Hudson, 1971), p.98.

(40) Edwin Muir, *Scott and Scotland* (George Routledge and Sons, Ltd., 1936), pp.151-52.

(41) *Memoirs of the Life of Sir Walter Scott, Bart 7 vols, Vol.2*, p.135.

(42) Walter Scott, *Kenilworth* (Penguin Books, 1999), p.50.

(43) *Familiar Letters of Sir Walter Scott 2 vols* (David Douglas, 1894), *Vol.1*, p.80.

(44) ⋯he [Scott] regarded the embarrassments of his commercial firm, on the whole, with the feelings not of a merchant but of a gentleman⋯He paid the penalty of health and life, but he saved his honour and his self-respect; "The glory dies not, and the grief is past." From *Memoirs of the Life of Sir Walter Scott, Bart 7 vols, Vol.6*, p.167.

(45) *Familiar Letters of Sir Walter Scott 2 vols* (David Douglas, 1894), *Vol.1*, p.72.

(46) Georg Wilhelm Friedrich Hegal, *Phänomenologie des Geistes*, (Nikol Verlagsges. mbH, 2021), pp.535-536.

(47) Hegel also published other important books, such as *Wissenschaft der Logik* (*Science of Logic*) between 1812-1816, and *Grundlinien der Philosophie des Rechts* (*The Outline of the Philosophy of Right*) in 1821, etc.

(48) *Phänomenologie des Geistes*, pp.140-141.

(49) Søren Kierkegaard, *Either/Or: A Fragment of Life* (Translated by Alastair Hannay, Penguin Books, 2004), p.52.

(50) Søren Kierkegaard, *The Sickness unto Death* (Translated by Alastair Hannay, Penguin

Books, 2004), p37.

(51) *Either/Or: A Fragment of Life*, p.54.

(52) Friedrich Nietzsche, *Also sprach Zarathustra* (Insel Klassik, 2011), p.315.

(53) *Ibid.*, p.96.

(54) Jean-Paul Sartre, *L'existentialisme est un humanisme* (Gallimard, 1996), p.26.

(55) *Ibid.*, p.77.

(56) Jean-Paul Sartre, *Qu'est-ce que la littérature ?* (Gallimard, 1948), p.294.

Königsberg Castle (1885)

# BIBLIOGRAPHY

Albert, Liv. *Greek Mythology: The Gods, Goddesses, and Heroes Handbook*, Adams Media, 2021.

Anderson, James, and G. Ross Roy. *Sir Walter Scott and History*, The Edina Press Lid., 1981.

Bacon, Francis. *Complete Essays of Francis Bacon*, Independently published, 2017.

Barness, Jonathan. *Aristotle: A Very Short Introduction*, Oxford University Press, 2000.

Belsey, Catherine. *Poststructuralism: A Very Short Introduction*, Oxford University Press, 2002.

Bowen, Zack. *Critical Essays on Sir Walter Scott: The Waverley Novels*, G. K. Hall & Co., 1996.

Captivating History Series. *History of France: A Captivating Guide to French History*, Captivating History, 2021.

———— *History of Scandinavia: A Captivating Guide to the History of Sweden, Norway, Denmark, Iceland, and Finland*, Captive History, 2023.

Clogg, Richard. *A Concise History of Greece*, Cambridge University Press, 2015.

Craig, Edward. *Philosophy: A Very Short Introduction*, Oxford University Press, 2020.

Crossway. *The Holy Bible, English Standard Version*, Crossway, a publishing ministry of Good News Publishers, 2001.

Danvers, Adrian. *Greek Mythology: A Timeless Collection of Greek Myths and Legends*, Dreamtime Books LLC, 2024.

Deighton, H. S. *The Oxford Introduction to British History: A Portrait of Britain*, Oxford University Press, 1987.

*Internet Encyclopedia of Philosophy*. iep.utm.edu

Fisher, Andrew, *Scotland, Third edition*, The Windrush Press, 1999.

Fullman, Joseph. *Ancient Civilizations*, Penguin Random House, 2013.

Jeffares, A. Norman. *Scott's Mind and Art*, Oliver & Boyd, 1969.

Johnson, Edgar. *Sir Walter Scott, The Great Unknown, Vol.1, Vol.2*, Hamish Hamilton, 1970.

Hawes, James. *The Shortest History of Germany*, The Experiment, LLC, 2019.

Hegal, Georg Wilhelm Friedrich. *Phänomenologie des Geistes*, Nikol Verlagsges. mbH, 2021.

Hirst, John. *The Shortest History of Europe*, The Experiment, LLC, 2022.

Hume, David. *David Hume Collection: A Treatise of Human Nature, An Enquiry Concerning Human Understanding, and Dialogues Concerning Natural Religion*, Independently published/Amazon.co.jp, 2020.

Kaye, Sharon. *Philosophy: A complete introduction*, Hodder & Stoughton, 2013.
————— *The Philosophy Book for Beginners: A Brief Introduction to Great Thinkers and Big Ideas*, Rockridge Press, 2021.
Kenny, Anthony. *A New History of Western Philosophy*, Oxford University Press, 2010.
Kierkegaard, Søren. *The Sickness unto Death* (Translated by Alastair Hannay), Penguin Books, 2004.
————— *Either/Or: A Fragment of Life* (Translated by Alastair Hannay), Penguin Books, 2004.
Locke, John. *Second Treatise of Government*, Independently published, 2014.
————— *An Essay Concerning Humane Understanding*, Independently published, 2019.
Lockhart, John Gibson. *The Life of Sir Walter Scott*, Hutchinson & Co., 1848.
Mackie, J. D., *A History of Scotland, Second edition*, Penguin Books, 1978.
Maclean, Fitzroy, *Scotland: A Concise History, Revised edition*, Thames and Hudson, 1993.
Nietzsche, Friedrich. *Also sprach Zarathustra*, Insel Klassik, 2011.
Nishino, Hiromichi. *The Future of English Spreading Around the World*, Ryutsu Keizai University Press, 2023.
————— *Discovering London in the 21$^{st}$ Century*, Ryutsu Keizai University Press, 2024.
Norgate, G. LE Grys. *The Life of Sir Walter Scott*, Methuen & CO., 1906.
Pearson, Hesketh. *Walter Scott: His Life and Personality*, Methuen & CO. Ltd., 1954.
Reed, James. *Sir Walter Scott: Landscape and Locality*, The Athlone Press, 1980.
Riches, John. *The Bible: A Very Short Introduction Second Edition*, Oxford University Press, 2021.
Russell, Bertrand. *History of Western Philosophy*, Routledge Classics, 1996.
Sartre, Jean-Paul. *L'existentialisme est un humanisme*, Gallimard, 1996.
————— *Qu'est-ce que la littérature ?*, Gallimard, 2008.
Scruton, Roger. *Kant: A Very Short Introduction*, Oxford University Press, 2001.
Shaw, Harry E. *Critical Essays on Sir Walter Scott: The Waverley Novels*, G. K. Hall & Co., 1996.
Stuart, Charles James. *The Holy Bible: Authorized King James Version*, Oxford University Press, 1993.
Sutherland, John. *The Life of Walter Scott*, Blackwell Publishers, 1995.
Taylor, Alfred Edward. *Plato: The Mind of Plato*, Diamond Books, 2017.
Taylor, C.C.W. *Socrates: A Very Short Introduction*, Oxford University Press, 2019.
Thonhause, Gerhard. *Heideggers "Sein und Zeit": Einführung und Kommentar*, J. B. Metzler, 2022.
Warburton, Nigel. *A Little History of Philosophy*, Yale University Press, 2011.
Wood, John Cunningham. *Karl Marx's Economics: Critical Assessments Volume I, II*, Croom Helm, 1988.
Walbank, Frank W. *Polybius, The Rise of the Roman Empire*, Penguin Books, 1979.
Wilson, A. N. *A Life of Walter Scott*, Mandarin, 1996.

# AFTERWORD

Originally, the core content of this book, which is about the history of Western philosophy, is made up of the paper 'A Study of the Future Vision of Philosophy — From the Perspective of the History of Western Philosophy' submitted to RYUTSU KEIZAI DAIGAKU RONSHU (The Journal of Ryutsu-Keizai University), Vol. 58, No.3, January 2023. Then, a detailed introduction and explanation of Greek mythology and Christianity, which form the basis of European civilization, have been added and compiled to provide a bird's-eye view of European history and culture. In addition, I introduced the ideas of William Wordsworth and Walter Scott, two of the opinion leaders of the English Romantics in the 19th century, which is also my field of expertise. This book aims to provide relevant information about European mythology, religion, philosophy, and literature.

As for the part about Wordsworth, I derived some contents, which I modified and added this time, from my two books - *The Future of English Spreading Around the World: A Brief History of English Language and Literature* (2023) and *Discovering London in the 21st Century* (2024). As for Scott's part, in my book *The Future of English Spreading Around the World*, I analyzed his sense of history. However, in this book, I tried to exhibit Scott's different perspective while maintaining the main concept. David Hume's article is also from *The Future of English Spreading Around the World* with rectifications added. Karl Marx's article is also a revised version of the previous book *Discovering London in the 21st Century*. Therefore, the thoughts and ideas of Wordsworth, Hume, and Marx overlap with the concept in the English books that I have written and published. I also briefly included the histories of Greece, the Roman Empire, France, England, Scotland, Germany, and Denmark that will help the readers to understand the diverse and conflicting ideas of the philosophers from each country. In addition, there are many contents in this book that overlap with what I have spoken about at cultural lectures that I have given to the general public in various places, what I have lectured at many universities, and what I have written in many books and magazines.

Most of the photographs used in this book (for example, portraits) are from the public domain. Furthermore, some of the photos were provided by me, the author of this book (p.128, p.138, p.140, p.145, p.146, p.147, p.148 above and below, p.151 below, p.156, p.160, p.222, p.223, and p.232). Others are from Mr. Yasumasa Nishino (p.13, p.41, p.92, p.102, p.103, p.104, p105 above, p.106 below, p.107 above and below, p.114, and p.200) and Mr. Takumi Matsuoka (p.55 above, p.91 above, p.162, and p.163 below). Unfortunately, I couldn't get a photo of Heidegger, so I used my own drawing of him for the portrait on page 205 instead. And I would like to take this opportunity to thank these two people for their help in writing this book: Mr. Kiyoshi Hirose and Mr. Atsufumi Nishino. Mr. Hirose is a former colleague of mine, a devout Christian, good at German, studied Hegel at the

graduate school of Waseda University and obtained a master's degree; Atsufumi is a young freelance writer with a deep understanding of philosophy.

I would like to thank all the staff involved in the production of this book for their cooperation. Finally, again, I would like to express my gratitude to Mr. Ei Onozaki of Ryutsu Keizai University Press.

Magnolia Blossom Vase

Hiromichi Nishino

# THE AUTHOR

**西野 博道**（にしの・ひろみち）

東京都出身。早稲田大学卒業、同専攻科修了、同大学院修士課程修了。専攻は英語英文学。現在、東京理科大学、東京未来大学、文教大学、茨城大学、流通経済大学ほか非常勤講師。著書に『イギリスの古城を旅する』（双葉社）『戦略戦術兵器事典⑤ヨーロッパ城郭編』（共著・学習研究社）『美神を追いて－イギリス・ロマン派の系譜』（共著・音羽書房鶴見書店）『21世紀イギリス文化を知る事典』（共著・東京書籍）『スコットランド文化事典』（共著・原書房）*The Future of English Spreading Around the World, Discovering London in the 21ˢᵗ Century*（流通経済大学出版会）のほか『埼玉の城址30選』（埼玉新聞社）『江戸城の縄張りをめぐる』（幹書房）『関東の城址を歩く』『英傑を生んだ日本の城址を歩く』（さきたま出版会）『日本の城郭－築城者の野望』『日本の城郭－名将のプライド』（柏書房）など日英城郭研究の成果を踏まえた著書が多数ある。'The History of Japanese Castles with the Perspective of British Castles'（流通經濟大學論集 2021.10）'A Study of the Future Vision of Philosophy — From the Perspective of the History of Western Philosophy'（流通經濟大學論集 2023.1）等はネット公開されているので是非ご覧ください。

## A Brief History of Western Culture and Philosophy

発行日　2025年3月1日　初版発行

著　者　西　野　博　道

発行者　片　山　直　登

発行所　流通経済大学出版会
　　　　〒301-8555　茨城県龍ヶ崎市120
　　　　電話　0297-60-1167　FAX　0297-60-1165

Printed in Japan/アベル社
ISBN978-4-911205-03-7 C0010 ¥1800E